ISO 14000

ISO 14000

THE BUSINESS MANAGER'S COMPLETE GUIDE TO ENVIRONMENTAL MANAGEMENT

PERRY JOHNSON

John Wiley & Sons, Inc.

New York ➤ Chichester ➤ Weinheim ➤ Brisbane ➤ Singapore ➤ Toronto

This text is printed on acid-free paper.

Copyright © 1997 by Perry Johnson
Published by John Wiley & Sons, Inc.

This publication is designed to provide accurate and authoritative
information in regard to the subject matter covered. It is sold
with the understanding that the publisher is not engaged in
rendering legal, accounting, or other professional services. If
legal advice or other expert assistance is required, the services
of a competent professional person should be sought.

Library of Congress Cataloging-in-Publication Data:

Johnson, Perry L. (Perry Lawrence), 1948–
    ISO 14000 : the business manager's complete guide to environmental
management / Perry Johnson.
        p.   cm.
    Includes bibliographical references and index.
    ISBN 0-471-16564-6 (cloth : alk. paper)
    1. ISO 14000 Series Standards.   2. Environmental protection—
Standards.   I. Title.
TS155.7.J64   1997
658.4'08—dc20   96-46082

Printed in the United States of America

10   9   8   7   6   5   4   3   2   1

Acknowledgments

Several trusted associates were responsible for the success of this project. While I do not have space to thank them all, some deserve special mention:

My staff and I could not have proceeded without the expert insight of Registrar Accreditation Board (RAB) chief executive officer Joseph Dunbeck and vice president of Conformity Assessment Paul Fortlage. Their knowledge of the intricacies of ISO 14000 implementation and registration was valuable every step of the way. They were also forthcoming with details about the National Accreditation Program, formed in conjunction with the American National Standards Institute (ANSI). Thanks also to John Donaldson, vice president for Conformity Assessment at ANSI.

Rod King, at the International Register of Certified Auditors (IRCA), and Roger Brockway, at the United Kingdom Accreditation Service (UKAS), both located in London, helped us wade through the maze of training organization accreditation requirements and explained how they would apply to the nascent ISO 14000 standard.

We owe a special debt of gratitude to Mary Jane Wilkinson, also of the United Kingdom Accreditation Service, who helped arrange several meetings with Mr. Brockway and made sure that our telephone calls were returned.

One of the important, emerging concepts in our field is international recognition of auditor credentials. Noel Matthews of the International Auditor Training and Certification Program (IATCA), in Canberra, Australia, explained patiently how major accrediting bodies might make the transition to offering IATCA certification.

Erik Bean, of the editorial staff at Perry Johnson, Inc., was instrumental in tying up loose ends. His dedication to this project is appreciated.

Editorial staff member Molly Dando conducted most of the research for this project.

This project required extensive use of library facilities, and the staff of the Shapiro Undergraduate Library at the University of Michigan-Ann Arbor. We wish to express our heartfelt appreciation to all of you at this time.

Special thanks to our Environmental Program Manager, Denise Seipke and contract consultants—Ralph Grover and Gene Michael—who provided technical expertise and clarified important points. Without your insight, patience, and persistence, this project would not have been possible.

PERRY L. JOHNSON

Southfield, Michigan
May 1997

Contents

Chapter 1: **The Value of Conformance**   **1**
Certifiably Green

Chapter 2: **Setting the Standard**   **27**

Chapter 3: **About ISO 14001**   **43**

Chapter 4: **Scope and Definitions**   **55**

Chapter 5: **ISO 14001**   **75**
Clause (Section) 4

Chapter 6: **Implementing Your Environmental
Management System**   **109**

Chapter 7: **Procedures**   **133**

Chapter 8: **Avoiding the Pitfalls**   **157**

Chapter 9: **The Internal Audit**   **169**

Chapter 10: **The Registration Audit**   **187**

Chapter 11: **Marketing Your Environmental Position**   **207**

Postscript: **The Business of Being Human**   **219**

Bibliography   **229**

Index   **233**

ISO 14000

Chapter 1

The Value of Conformance

Certifiably Green

ISO 14000 is a system that will essentially revitalize environmental regulation.

—JAMES M. SEIF, Secretary
U.S. Department of Environmental Protection

Whether you are a shareholder, general manager, chief executive, strategic planner, or the person in your organization who was tossed this book and told to look into ISO 14000, you have the same essential questions: What's the bottom line? Are the benefits to my company worth our time, resources, and attention? Are there any risks associated with certification?

The benefits of conformance are immense: ISO 14000 builds a single global management system that will allow you to effectively manage your environmental responsibilities, reduce liability, and control costs, document your commitment to government, and promote your concern for the public.

With these benefits in mind, you still may ask: What will happen to my company, and our competitive position, if I ignore ISO 14000?

Worst-case scenarios can be summed up in words like Exxon *Valdez*, Three Mile Island, Chernobyl, Bhopal Chemical, Love Canal. These are the ultimate environmental disasters that can cripple even a major corporation, draw pickets to your doorstep, bog you down in endless litigation, initiate widespread boycotts of your products and cost you millions.

And if you say this can't happen to your company, consider Perrier: What could be safer than selling bottled water? Yet the discovery of traces of benzene in Perrier's water created a great crisis for this small company. Profits plummeted 75 percent in a single year, and the publicity contaminated 90 years of name recognition.

Such events are not acts of God beyond the scope of business control. The companies involved could have avoided many of these disasters if clearly defined environmental management systems like ISO 14000 had been in place. The worst example is possibly the most illustrative. The Exxon *Valdez* collided with a reef in Prince William Sound, Alaska. The resulting oil spill has cost Exxon upward of $3 billion in after-tax costs for cleanup, settlements, and legal penalties. It cost far more as customers publicly cut up their Exxon credit cards, and investors took Exxon off their preferred lists. Among the many factors revealed at the trial was that the skipper of the *Valdez* was under tremendous pressure to cut operating costs, and decided to risk the shallow waters because there was ice in the main shipping channel. He figured he could cut three miles from this run. And because there were no clear environmental management guidelines to red-flag it, a three-mile shortcut converged with other events and resulted in a multibillion-dollar cost.

This is a dramatic example of what can go wrong when the proper guidelines don't exist. How much is the lack of an effective environmental management system (EMS) already costing your company:

➤ In missed opportunities to reduce energy consumption and material waste?

➤ In administrative staff to address the literally thousands of environmental regulations in the United States, and in every country where you do business?

➤ In fines and penalties through government audits because your environmental aspects are out of compliance?

➤ In loss of confidence by stockholders and financial institutions who are unsure of your environmental risk factor?

➤ In poor public image, and in lost opportunities to delineate your product to those who prefer buying environmentally correct products—now a large segment of the population?

If you do not have an effective, companywide environmental management system in place, chances are you are not controlling these costs and, may in fact, be unsure how to adequately access or measure your actual environmental costs.

The task of management is to control internal costs and maximize market opportunities by enhancing your product and company image. Environmental stewardship, like quality, health, and safety, is a definable process that can yield immense benefits if managed. To have confidence in quality, for example, you establish a systemic approach like ISO 9000 or total quality management (TQM) to define, measure, and control the variables, thus assuring the outcomes as you have defined them. Environmental responsibilities—while broader and seemingly more nebulous—can just as readily respond to this approach.

Perhaps most importantly, to have confidence that you can avoid worst-case scenarios, reduce risk and liability, your leadership team must *control* the process. This is the real strength of ISO 14000. Measures are taken to eliminate the root cause of pollution. ISO 14000 has all the process controls built in, including measurement, preventive action, benchmarking, performance standards, and continuous improvement. This is nearly identical to the stance ISO 9000 and TQM have taken with quality. Instead of reacting after a problem emerges, you control the process, and ultimately the outcome. Previously hidden costs are revealed, allowing you to assess cost-benefit ratios.

■ A MANAGEMENT TOOL

ISO 14000 is a voluntary management tool developed by the international business community to provide companies with methodically structured and disciplined control over all aspects of their environmental impacts. This system allows your business to avoid risks and costly confusion, by incorporating environmental controls into your daily operations in a consistent, predictable, and cost-effective manner as you define identified needs.

With ISO 14000, your organization can establish policies based on your own assessment of the environmental aspects of your company's business and the environmental goals you have set. ISO 14000 does not mandate environmental performance beyond management's commitment, compliance to existing regulations, and a dedication to continuous improvement.

No two companies, even in the same field and with nearly identical products, are likely to have identical ISO 14000 programs. This versatility allows management to flexibly manage their environmental programs rather than adhere to mandated, restrictive compliance designed to meet detailed outcomes. With ISO 14000, the focus is on your specific environmental needs, as defined by your own evaluation. With ISO 14000, you are singularly concerned with the steps your own company takes.

➤ Designed for and by Business

The emphasis on flexibility is rooted in the origin of the standard. The International Organization for Standardization (I.S.O.) is headquartered in Geneva, Switzerland. Representatives from business in over 100 countries collaborate to create management standards with the widest possible input from world-wide businesses and organizations. ISO has an outstanding record of developing such voluntary standards, including ISO 9000 for quality management, ISO 9660 for standardized CD-ROM formatting, and more than a hundred other widely used standards.

The ISO 14000 standards emerged because of the need for management to gain some control over the chaotic and often contradictory environmental regulations that exist from one country to the next and indeed, from one state to the next. This total lack of uniformity complicates global business and, more often than not, acts as an unofficial defacto barrier to free and open trade.

➤ Global Acceptance

The enthusiasm for developing these new world standards has been unprecedented. From England to Australia, and from Sweden to South Korea, the international business community is embracing ISO 14000. In fact, to date 113 countries have endorsed ISO 14000.

In some countries, ISO 14000 has become a requirement for doing business. Already, the European Union has regulations in place to force the use of ISO 14000. The governments of Germany, Great Britain, the Netherlands, Norway, and the Philippines, and agencies of the U.S. government, may soon only do business with companies that have environmental management systems in place. The European Union has adopted ISO 14000 as its sole EMS standard under the name EN 14001. It replaces the *Eco-Management and Audit Scheme* (EMAS).

The *Japanese Accreditation Board* (JAB) started EMS accreditation activities in June 1996 and as of October 1996 more than 100 facilities there had achieved certification either to ISO 14001 or another EMS standard.

Even before ISO 14000 was released by the International Organization for Standardization in September 1996, fifty companies had committed to it. Multinational corporations such as SGS Thomson, Hitachi, Fuji Electric Company Ltd., Bristol Myers, Ford, Volvo, Rockwell International, Sony, and Toshiba Corporation were among the first companies to take up this new management tool.

They see ISO 14000 as a means of expanding global markets and reducing the risks entailed by multiple, often conflicting, environmental regulations. Chuck Reich, a 3M division vice president who has already initiated ISO 14000 implementation, expresses the hope of most company leaders when he says, "As more companies come on board, more people will understand the benefits of certified, consistent standards. In this way, we can have a common set of environmental standards throughout the world, and finally will discourage environmental issues from becoming trade barriers."

Canon, Inc., which operates in more than 130 countries, realized it was necessary to follow responsible environmental ethics to maintain market competitiveness. That company achieved conformance with an ISO 14000 precursor in September 1994, and expected 30 facilities to become ISO 14000-registered by the end of 1996.

The benefits, according to Canon, Inc.'s Environmental Audit Department Manager, Yasufumi Sato, include reducing energy consumption 25 percent by the year 2000. He says that goal is well within reach.

Governments everywhere, in fact, are recognizing that the traditional "command and control" approach to environmental regulation has not produced the desired results. Setting specific acts in regulatory stone has often led to regulating inconsequential aspects of an industry, while allowing grave ecological risk to remain unchecked in others. And as new scientific evidence about the environment becomes available, rigid regulations cannot be quickly adapted to meet needs. As Wilma Delaney of Dow Chemical Company has said, "We're not looking to roll back regulations. But we want the flexibility to meet the goals in the most cost-effective manner."

■ ATTITUDE CHANGE

ISO 14000 is a way of empowering businesses to take control of environmental responsibility and encouraging governments to approach the challenge with far greater flexibility.

Already, the Netherlands has demonstrated what can be done when government sets the goal, and looks to business to develop its own creative solutions. And in the United States, the Environmental Protection Agency has developed what it calls Project XL (eXcellence in Leadership), an effort that allows companies with demonstrated leadership in pollution control to operate under lower requirements than the law provides, with the company's guarantee it will strive to go beyond current standards. Intel and 3M have been the first to avail themselves of this opportunity. The XL program represents a genuine turning point in allowing business to take the lead.

Yet even without radical changes in government oversight, a company's conformance with ISO 14000 demonstrates to government agencies that it is committed to being proactive in environmental management, which leads to better working cooperation and communication, and makes your organization far less vulnerable to fines and public penalties. Since being out of compliance with even one EPA regulation can cost a company about $25,000 a day (and subject your management team to criminal prosecution), developing a working relationship, as well as government's and public respect for your company's integrity and commitment to the environment, can become a pocketbook objective.

The Department of Justice may consider ISO 14001 as proof of "best management practices." One analyst reports that "ISO 14001 may become the recognized standard that the Department of Justice looks to when determining if a company that had an accident did everything within its control to avoid the accident." Thus a company could avoid criminal prosecution, even if held civilly responsible.

These are the intangibles of ISO 14000 that do not fit neatly into cost-benefit equations. It is impossible to tally the citations that are not written, the lawsuits not filed, the fines not levied, the cost of accidents avoided because you have a credible system in place.

■ UNIVERSAL APPROACH

Now, if all this implies that ISO 14000 relates entirely to massive, global companies, that is simply not the case. The standard states: "It has been written to be applicable to all types and sizes of organizations and to accommodate diverse geographical, cultural and social conditions." Even small, nonmanufacturing companies that are decidedly local are embracing ISO 14000 because, while they may confine their operations to one country, their partners in joint ventures and alliances do not. In the web of today's business relationships, most companies are partners or suppliers to larger, international corporations.

They see the necessity to live up to customer specifications. Major companies and government purchasing agencies alike are discussing ways to require ISO 14000 participation as a condition of being a first-tier supplier (similiar to the Big 3's mandate for QS9000, the automotive quality standard). ISO 14000 can thus be central to a growth strategy that gives your organization access to global alliances and new markets.

Ford Motor Company is one of industry's leaders in adopting ISO 14001. Graham Chatburn, Ford's environment manager, who was also a member of the technical committee that designed ISO 14000, says, "Ford has no plans to require that all of our suppliers adopt ISO 14000, yet our suppliers typically follow our lead. They know Ford Motor Company doesn't commit to an effort of this magnitude unless it is good business. And what's good business for us, is good business for those who serve us as well."

■ GOOD BUSINESS

ISO 14000 is "good business" because it can lead to greater efficiencies and reduce materials and operating costs. The very definition of "environment" is all-inclusive: It means anything that consumes energy and produces waste.

Environmental issues span the entire management spectrum—material costs, productivity, quality, liability, health, and safety. An efficient and cost-effective systems approach to managing these variables of doing business impacts bottom-line profitability. Thus ISO 14000 inspires a shift in thinking that takes environmental management out of the expense side of the ledger, and places it where it belongs, as a direct and indirect producer of income.

Most companies' experience in quality management over the past decade should demonstrate what is possible with a viable environmental management systems control approach, like ISO 14000. It came as a revelation to most businesses that if they incorporated quality into the entire process, rather than inspecting it in at the end of the assembly line, immense savings were possible. Companies learned, in fact, that quality is free: If you place the right controls into your process, those controls will reduce waste and improve productivity far beyond the initial cost of the change. Quality can be free, and with systemic control, environmental stewardship often can be, also.

There are far too many examples of environmental stewardship paying dividends to list here. On a small scale, American Express recently installed energy-saving lighting in its 51-story Manhattan headquarters building, saving more than 40 percent on its electric bills. On a larger scale, Jerai International Park is developing a planned community in northern Malaysia that will utilize solid and liquid wastes to generate electricity through incineration and digestion, making JIP's planned city entirely energy self-sufficient.

For the past 20 years, 3M, a leader in environmental management, has focused the organization's attention in a program called Pollution Prevention Pays. More than 4,000 improvements have resulted, eliminating 1.3 billion pounds of pollutants, while saving 3M more than $710 million, and greatly enhancing the company's public image.

The 10-year effort by Xerox to establish waste-free products, factories, and offices has not only produced tremendous savings, but earned the company numerous awards for outstanding public service. As Paul Allaire, Chairman and CEO of Xerox, has said, "The notion that what is good for the environment is good for business is proving to be true at Xerox."

➤ Eco-Efficient Companies Do Better

Numerous studies bear out Allaire's conclusion. The World Business Council for Sustainable Development, an international organization of 120 leading corporations, concluded, "Eco-efficient companies are better managed companies, and better managed companies are the most successful."

Other studies confirm the bottom-line benefits of environmental management. The *Green Business Letter,* for example, compared *Fortune Magazine*'s overall ranking for the most profitable companies and found that 9 of the top 10 also ranked among the top 10 percent of companies for environmental and community responsibility. A more comprehensive study by Stuart Hart of the University of Michigan Business School, analyzed the effects of pollution reduction compared with financial performance of 127 companies from the Standard & Poor's 500 stock list. He concluded that environmental actions, far from acting as cost penalties, actually increased profitability, and that a company typically could save money during its first 70 percent of pollution reductions without reaching a point of diminishing returns.

Some industries, such as the American automotive industry, actually became more competitive when challenged to meet environmental and energy standards. Germany's leaders are convinced that environmental efforts actually stimulate business by challenging companies to be more innovative and creative in developing new technologies. Technologies, they add, actually create entirely new markets.

So the arguments against environmental action are no longer believable, and evidence that corporate environmental stewardship pays is plentiful.

➤ Investors Expect an Environmental Management System

The success of companies that manage their environmental aspects represents more than the obvious cost savings of increased efficiency and reduced waste; it reflects a concerned investment community. Certification under a program like ISO 14001 assures investors that you are in control, which enhances stock value, and improves your ability to obtain capital.

Increasingly, if your company cannot assure the financial community that you are in control of environmental risks, then your lending institution may suggest you look elsewhere. As of 1995, more than 74 private banks from around the world had signed a statement that commitment to environmental protection would be evaluated in lending practices. And the World Bank, which is the central support for multilateral development banks, has maintained a policy of evaluating proposals heavily based on environmental management. From the corner branch of your local bank to the

World Bank, your company's environmental controls will define your potential to raise capital.

Credit rating companies are assisting the lending industry in its efforts to finance only those operations with definable and controlled environmental risks. TransUnion, one of the United State's leading credit-reporting agencies, is providing environmental reporting as part of its normal services to financial institutions across the country. It is working from a database that includes more than seven million federal, state, and county environmental records. Rick Lunch, vice president of TransUnion, explains, "Lenders need to know what their potential risk exposure on a loan is. A growing concern in the lending community is environmental liability."

In this information age, the financial community has no dearth of resources to examine your company's environmental history and current practices. The Environmental Bankers Association, with major commercial bank members, now acts as a clearinghouse for information on companies and their environmental efforts.

How well you manage your environmental aspects may also impact your company's insurance premiums. In 1996, major insurance carriers met with 35 different companies and representatives of the Environmental Protection Agency to discuss ways to give reduced rates to companies who can prove environmental responsibility, including ISO 14001 certification. On the international scene, insurance carriers, including industry leaders like Lloyd's of London and Munich Re, are seen in attendance at international environmental management conferences.

Yet it goes further, all the way to Wall Street, in fact. Environmental investors are becoming a significant faction in the investor community. A number of companies sponsor "green" investments: Socially Responsible Investing (SRI),

Business Ethics, Co-op America, the Green Money Journal, and others. Some mutual fund companies, such as the Calvert Group, invest their funds entirely in companies that can consistently demonstrate environmental responsibility. And banks are even offering EcoDeposit accounts, which are IRAs, CDs, and money markets that focus on environmentally responsible companies.

➤ Good Corporate Citizenship: A Marketing Tool

Many companies use their environmental responsibility as a badge of distinction and provide consumers another reason for buying their products. They seek out, display, and promote seals of certification and environmentally-proactive labels. This is especially useful in crowded markets, where it is more difficult to define a product based on quality and cost alone. Other considerations, like concern for the environment, can make a difference in such markets and, in fact, can be the deciding purchasing factor. This has been documented by Indianapolis-based Walker Information Co.

Companies like Ben & Jerry's and Bath & Body Works are known for their proactive environmental position and have already opened their records up to objective third party audits. Other companies that promote their ecological stance include Arm & Hammer, AT&T, Federal Express, Hallmark, Home Depot, Honeywell, Levi Strauss, Polaroid, Reebok, Target Stores, Texas Instruments, Time Warner, Viacom, and Xerox. The consensus among these companies is that environmental stewardship is a marketable commodity.

While these companies and investment organizations represent more of a growing trend than a mainstream reality, most investors today are influenced by a company's environmental management record. Growing numbers of the financial community are monitoring environmental performance as a fundamental investment criterion.

It's not enough to just put on a show. Twenty years ago, a company could have its employees switch from Styrofoam to ceramic coffee mugs and get front-page applause for this effort. Today, governments and the public are demanding high levels of disclosure of company activities as they relate to energy and the environment.

In the United States, the Superfund Amendments and Reauthorization Act, also known as the "Right-to-Know Act," requires that companies report all hazardous substances they introduce to air, water, or land. This law gives reporters and stock analysts alike ample information for evaluating any company's environmental efforts.

➤ No Place to Hide

Such disclosure laws form the basis for organizations like Corporate Environmental Data Clearinghouse (CEDC), which evaluates numerous aspects of a company's environmental activities, not only the technical details of energy and waste management, but data on penalties and citations, pending litigation, and how much a company is spending on lobbyists and anti-environmental politicians. From this information, newspapers and magazines publish lists such as "Europe's Top Polluters," "America's Toxic Ten," and the "World's 12 Worst Corporate Citizens."

Increased public exposure negates "greenwashing"—the massive advertising investments companies make each year to improve their environmental images. One publication, for example, took the occasion of Rockwell's environmental advertising campaign, which used Ansel Adams's nature photography, to list the 166 separate hazardous-waste dumps and $18.5 million in fines for environmental violations Rockwell had incurred. Today with disclosure laws and instantaneous electronic communications, companies must prove they are not just "talking the talk" but "walking the walk."

■ THE VALUE OF A POSITIVE IMAGE

Environmental management can have a significant public relations and marketing payoff. Through ISO 14001 certification, you can demonstrate objective proof that your company is a concerned and caring environmental steward. American companies spend about half of their entire budgets in advertising, and this promotional material makes a difference.

Companies working to become ISO 14000 conformant find they gain many surprising benefits with development in that direction. Your employees want to take pride in their work and their company, and social responsibility enhances that pride. Feeling good about your company leads to company loyalty, far less employee turnover, and improved employment recruiting; surveys show that the most talented and intelligent young people prefer to join environmentally responsible companies.

An even more fundamental reason for investing in an environmental management system like ISO 14000 is that your customers may demand it. Study after study in Europe and the United States demonstrates that most people today see themselves as concerned about the environment. Indeed, surveys in both America and Europe show that as many as 56 percent of the buying public has rejected one product and purchased another solely on the basis of environmental considerations.

Emerging markets often have the highest environmental expectations. Asia, with its dense population and tradition of naturalism, is becoming an environmental leader. The strictest environmental regulations in the world are in effect in Japan. And Japan's largest conglomerates—Toyota, Sony, Chemical Ricoh, Canon, Fujitsu, and Nippon Petroleum—all are already certified to ISO 14001. Elsewhere in Asia, Thailand's 10 largest corporations are already implementing ISO 14001. The People's Republic of China, with a quarter of the world's population, is taking initial steps into the industrial community; it is embracing the United Nations' Agenda 21's environmental guidelines and committed to growth that is in harmony with its environmentally sensitive culture.

Everywhere, the environment has become an all-pervasive issue that affects every aspect of our lives, at home and on the job in our communities, in our towns and states, and in national and international forums. As individuals, each of us in the corporate world should feel a personal responsibility to add to, or at least not to detract from, the environment in which we operate.

This environmental consciousness is a tremendous asset in establishing and maintaining an effort like ISO 14000. Employees take up the effort enthusiastically and take personal and professional pride in knowing that their efforts are not just right for your company, but right for their ethics and beliefs. Unions are equally enthusiastic as long as they are convinced management is committed, and this isn't another "program of the week." Union leaders say they are for ISO 14000 because it is environmentally responsible, and touches on health and safety. Equally important, increased efficiencies can actually save jobs.

One of the best demonstrations of enthusiasm for environmental action can be seen in the auto industry's elimination of chlorofluorocarbons (CFCs), from their products and plants.

Once it was established that CFCs were a genuine threat to the ozone layer of the atmosphere, companies reengineered their products to do away with this coolant a full two years ahead of regulated deadlines. Jack Smith, General Motors Chairman, said, "I was thoroughly impressed in how this effort revealed deeply felt commitment on everyone's part. Everyone was working not because of impending regulations, but for results."

This chapter began by stressing the importance of management gaining control of the process to assure results. But results do not come from mandates from the boardroom alone. General Dwight D. Eisenhower, when he first became President of the United States, said, "I'm sitting here at a great big desk with lots of buttons on it, but the buttons aren't connected to anything. To get anything done, I have to get out from behind that desk and convince everyone." Eisenhower was right. Everyone in the organization has to buy into a direction, and experience some sense of ownership, roll up their sleeves and pitch in for any genuine change to take place.

■ EMPOWERING EMPLOYEES LEADS TO SUCCESS

One of ISO 14000's greatest strengths is that it establishes a process that spreads responsibility and participation to every individual on every staff within your organization. This is the same experience of companies that developed quality systems under ISO 9000. Quality, they discovered, was too important to be left to a cadre of quality control inspectors. Only when everyone became quality conscious and became part of the process, did quality suddenly and dramatically improve. Since ISO 14000 is closely patterned after the successful ISO 9000, the same experience should result.

What ISO 14000 can do is effectively tear down the barriers between environmental coordinators charged with compliance responsibility and those employees with daily operating responsibility. Environmental coordinators simply had no personal authority to facilitate behavioral changes. Their job was to monitor emmissions and discharges and report to government agencies.

ISO 14000 removes the walls and empowers individuals within an organization. By elevating environmental management to a corporatewide concern, equal to financial and quality concerns, the environmental coordinator manages control of environmental aspects and facilitates change. The function is connected to and dependent on every area, department, and work group. Support is further assured as ISO 14000 training teaches employees the effect on the environment of their own work duties, how these can be minimized, what the benefit is for conformance and what the negative consequences can be if responsibilities are ignored. Environmental management is written into job descriptions, and becomes part of evaluations and incentives. It becomes everyone's task, everyone's personal responsibility.

Consider that Fluke Corporation, an international electronics company, already had an active environmental management department before it began to merge current operations with ISO 14001 guidelines. Once managers began talking to each other about environmental costs, potential savings began emerging. The people in manufacturing began talking to the waste treatment people. They discovered that the air scrubbers used up to four million gallons of water a month. They worked out a way to recycle the wastewater dramatically reducing plant water use and saved the company $216,000 a year. George Bissonette, Fluke's environmental, health and safety manager, concluded: "Corporate, operational and environmental people can become separated from the rest of the organization. The resulting lack of cooperation really creates a communications gap that leads to missed improvements, and noncompliance. One of ISO 14001's greatest payoffs to me is that it leads to effective communications."

Branda Lang is a quality assurance supervisor at Millar Western Pulp, which has recently been implementing ISO 14001. She said, "Employees started realizing that the department I work in does have an impact on other departments and the whole company. Everyone soon understood that ISO 14001 wasn't just another program. It was part of the way we live."

Total integration of environmental responsibility into the existing operation is the essence of ISO 14000. You are, in effect, weaving environmental stewardship into the very fabric of your organizational life. And one of the savings is that ISO 14000 allows you the flexibility to retain your existing culture, without tossing out everything else. The best clothes are ones that are tailor-made for you, and with ISO 14000 you are the tailor.

Environmental controls involve everyone, and virtually everyone seems conscious of their personal and professional responsibility. It is impossible to exaggerate the power of environmental concern. This highly personal involvement means environmental awareness. It means, too, that your company's stewardship is fast becoming a critical factor in how your stockholders, government regulators, competitors, employees, customers, and the public view your company's performance as a responsible corporate citizen.

The bottom line is that environmental management is in your company's best interest, both from the downside view of avoiding liability and dealing with the likelihood of even more rigid regulations, and from the upside view of cost-efficient management control, good investor and public relations, and a powerful motivating tool for your own employees.

■ WHY THIS ENVIRONMENTAL MANAGEMENT SYSTEM?

Even if there is ample proof that an environmental management system is essential, the question remains—why ISO 14000?

The answer is that it was developed by businesspeople, as a market-driven approach that allows you maximum control over your business decisions.

ISO 14000 is the most flexible approach to environmental oversight yet devised. It allows you to critically review existing operations and bring them into conformance with your standards. The system challenges your organization to set up an effective structure to accomplish environmental improvements; public communication is built into the system and continuous improvement is assured.

Another answer is that ISO 14000 makes use of methods that have already been tested and found effective.

Many of the procedures of ISO 14000 are identical to those of the already established ISO 9000 quality standards. The same document control, management reviews, and internal audits apply to both. Companies estimate that those who already have ISO 9000 structures in place can save up to 50 percent compared with designing a uniquely new system.

Indeed, ISO 14000 conforms to virtually all total quality management approaches in structure and application. So it is relatively simple to integrate ISO 14000 into existing quality, health, and safety systems. As Steve Kopp describes Global

Metallurgical's approach, "Employees don't want to be responsible for learning and maintaining several sets of procedures, therefore, where it is appropriate, environmental, quality and safety concerns have been integrated into training and work instructions." ISO 14000 makes a holistic approach possible.

Yet another answer is that ISO 14000 is destined to become the new standard for business everywhere. For example, when the ISO Environmental Management System Technical Committee met in Oslo, Norway, in 1996, more than 500 delegates representing 43 of the largest, most industrialized nations on earth, participated. That was the largest attendance ever for an ISO technical committee and demonstrated the worldwide interest and support for this new approach.

■ AGILITY IS EVERYTHING

Because the major companies and countries of the world are in full support of the standards, the lack of ISO 14000 certification might well handicap your organization. When Greenpeace made global headlines by decrying the fact that dolphins were dying in tuna nets, Starkist reacted rapidly, improving the nets and advertising their product as "Dolphin Safe." Other canned tuna companies followed suit, but they never regained the market share lost to Starkist. If you wait for proof that ISO 14000 is both vital and effective before getting involved, you may have waited too long. Respected environmental journalist Joel Makower concisely analyzed the result of a reactionary position: "Companies that wait and hope that environmental responsibility all goes away will be bypassed and outclassed by their more enlightened competitors."

ISO 14000 is not a panacea. It is not greenwashing that gives the appearance of responsibility without actual commitment. ISO 14000 is only an assurance that a company is striving to comply with regulatory requirements and achieving self-defined goals. Yet with genuine leadership commitment, ISO 14000 will allow your organization to live up to environmental stewardship.

And it will allow you to live with the uncertainty of what lies ahead. The CFC experience points out yet another critical factor in considering your company's environmental approach: No one can anticipate how new scientific findings about the environment will impact your future business. CFCs were considered the most effective refrigerant until ozone research proved they were dangerous.

We are at the threshold of the environmental age, just stepping into an era of discovery that is certain to challenge virtually every aspect of how we live and work and even play together. Companies need to have an environmental management system in place that is agile enough to respond to rapid and radically changing technology and needs. As one corporate executive put it, "having an environmental management system like ISO 14001 is like buying insurance for the future on an installment plan."

This opening, defining chapter has provided abundant evidence that we are entering a new era in global business, which will require a new kind of leadership.

Peter Drucker, in his book *New Realities*, says that traditional leaders organized around issues, and disagreed over ends. The issue of environmental stewardship—is already being defined for us. The new leadership must focus not on determining "ends," but on developing the most reasonable "means" to achieve socially responsible ends. ISO 14000 is not an end, but a reasonable and responsive means—a tool—for achieving environmental ends.

Chapter

Setting the Standard

There is something fundamentally wrong in treating the earth as if it were a business in liquidation.

—HERMAN DALY
World Bank

I SO 14000 is more than a new global system for environmental management. It may well represent a pivotal point in the relationship between business, government, environmentalists, and the public. It has the potential to set aside the long-perceived image of businesses as the "spoilers," and give us the opportunity to become proactive partners in a new, and more productive, era of ecosystem management.

Before a U.S. Senate committee, James M. Seif, Secretary, Department of Environmental Protection, captured the importance of this event: "ISO 14000 represents a market-driven approach to environmental protection that is potentially many times more effective in achieving significant environmental improvements than traditional 'command and control' regulatory methods have become.

"These new tools approach environmental protection in an entirely new way, using performance-based objectives, positive incentives to comply, external validation, a flexible approach to implementation and systems which constantly looks for new opportunities to prevent pollution and reduce environmental compliance costs," Seif concluded, "ISO 14000 is a system that will essentially privatize environmental regulation."

To understand the profound implications of this opportunity, it is essential to review the brief history of environmental management. For the evolution has taken several significant steps, and some missteps, before arriving at this new juncture.

In the 1960s, the concern for the environment degradation began to approach a true international mass movement. Many say it began with a book, Rachel Carson's *Silent Spring*, that was published in 1962. More than a exposé on the pesticides industry, *Silent Spring* was a scathing indictment of all business and industry as irresponsible opportunists. Business was depicted as the arch villain in this unfolding environmental drama.

■ A TURNING POINT

By the 1960s, the world's population had doubled, and industrialization had increased by a factor of 50—the largest part of that increase in the booming 1950s. Up until that point, neither by numbers nor by technology, had the human race measured or monitored their permanent impact on the planet's ecosystem. In business terms, the earth's vast resources and rejuvenating powers were like a bank account that was so large and self-sustaining that our species could live off the interest alone, never significantly drawing on the principal. But by the 1960s, it was becoming apparent that the drain in terms of population increases, energy consumption, and waste accumulation, had passed the point where what we were doing actually could have major, and potentially fatal, consequences. Up until then, business assumed that anything without a price tag attached was free. We were spending earth's assets faster than nature could regenerate them.

Business and industry largely ignored early expressions of concern as "questionable sources." Environmentalists were viewed by business as people who would prevent business activity, who would stand in the way of innovation and expansion, and who would inhibit a free and flexible market economy. As environmental author Joel Makower put it, "Business was more interested in saving the day, than in saving the planet."

Yet public awareness of earth's degradation continued to grow. It seemed to reach a societal crest in December of 1968 when the first photographs of earth from beyond the moon came back. Archibald Macleish wrote in the *New York Times*— "To see the earth as it truly is, small blue and beautiful in the eternal silence where it floats, is to see ourselves as riders on the earth together." People became keenly aware of the finite nature of our planet. They began speaking in terms of responsibility for "spaceship earth." And the inventor of the geodesic dome, Buckminster Fuller, captured the mood when he said, "The thing we discovered about spaceship earth is that it did not come with an owner's manual."

At the same time, there emerged a belief that only government was capable of solving environmental, and in fact, all societal problems. Business, after all, critics said, was Machiavellian and shortsighted, or as one commentator put it: "Business has the mentality of a child in the second grade. If you ask a second grader to choose between eternal life and recess, eternal life doesn't stand a chance. If you ask business to choose between a long-term sustainable future or good quarterly returns, the future doesn't stand a chance."

Business seemed to confirm this assessment by resisting all proposed changes as "inflationary," and repeatedly saying "it can't be done," fostering an adversarial relationship against any intervention by government or the environmentalists. Ironically, because of the rapid increase in electronic control and sensor technologies, business was actually able to do what even its leaders honestly thought was impossible. The American auto industry was the best example. The Big Three repeatedly testified before Congress that the technology to meet significant reductions in vehicular and stationary plant emissions didn't exist, and it would take decades to develop it. Yet when government passed the Clean Air Act, the automakers quickly hired aerospace engineers and borrowed their advanced electronic control systems, meeting every "impossible" federal standard. This was a Herculean effort, but to the public, business seemed to be stonewalling and thus, it lost credibility.

Meanwhile, environmental concern reached global dimensions: The unique characteristic of this new environmental movement was that it was both worldwide and universally centered on government regulation as the vehicle for change. Not only in the United States and Europe, but in the Communist world, and in emerging nations as well, an almost spontaneous popular movement was seeking political recourse for environmental improvement.

In Europe, green political parties emerged. Green party candidates had significant success in the 1980s in Germany, and the green party reached its peak in Great Britain when in 1989, the party won nearly 15 percent of the vote. Antienvironmental detractors said that the failure of green parties showed a peaking of interest, but just the opposite had happened. The green parties had served their purpose as the mainstream political parties took up virtually all the issues and green party planks, stealing their thunder and reason for existence. Survey after survey showed that most people in the United States and Europe saw themselves as environmentalists who wanted more government oversight of business, not less.

■ COMMAND AND CONTROL

With a mandate from the public, governments evolved a strategy of command and control, defining highly specific regulations with rigid measures, then requiring a stream of paperwork as proof of compliance. This process, which continues unabated today, creates a tremendous burden on industry. General Motors Chairman Roger Smith made this point in 1987 by calculating that if he stacked all the compliance paperwork in a single pile, it would be 42 stories high, would consume 10,000 acres of rain forests, and require 500 people working full time just to do the paperwork. And that was just for one company, one year.

Today in the United States, the combined command and control mechanisms of federal, state, and local pollution regulations have proven nearly impossible to manage. The federal share alone, according to the *Federal Register*, takes 20,000 pages to detail more than 10,000 environmental laws, and many calculate there are at least as many state and local regulations. In the United States alone, it was estimated by the late 1980s that business was spending more than $120 billion a year on regulatory compliance. And no one could calculate the additional burden of overlapping state and local regulations, or even the cost of federal regulations that often contradicted the rulings of other independent agencies.

The regulatory era was realizing the worst fears of business, creating an unprecedented burden on productivity and a massive hidden tax on all commerce. The cost of simply staying abreast of energy and environmental regulations had become a drain on companies' manpower, time, and limited resources. Too often, smaller companies have deemed it more cost-effective to ignore all regulations until a federal agent shows up and fines them for violations.

Command and control strategies have not been effective in solving environmental protection problems. The scope and impact of environmental degradation is increasing in some areas. The problem, some believe, is inefficient government oversight. Constantly changing regulations meant that companies have had to focus primarily on paper targets, not on long-term solutions to the underlying problems.

Recent studies by the Environmental Protection Agency, in fact, show that government regulations set limits and require conformance to the wrong things, when changes in other areas, or alternative approaches to the same problem, could actually eliminate more pollution at far lower costs. A case in point is the EPA specifications for reducing benzene emissions from oil refinery wastewater treatment plants. Dow Chemical came up with its own approach, which would have eliminated four times as much benzene at a cost of $6 million, yet the EPA's stringent rules required a less efficient process that cost five times as much. Inflexibility can severely impede environmental improvements.

The strategy of command and control also has not worked for government. It requires a virtual army of bureaucrats to police a vast set of imposed standards. Yet in an era of intense global competition, great pressures are exerted on government to reduce government agency staffing to balance budgets and deal with staggering federal deficits. To reduce federal staffing while maintaining a command and control philosophy meant that companies only complying under duress, could now slip through the process, making compliance impossible.

The failure of command and control regulation was most evident in the Communist countries that used absolute government powers in attempting to regulate the environment. When the Berlin Wall fell, and the world saw the condition of Eastern Europe's ecosystem, everyone was appalled. Environmental degradation in Soviet industrial communities was so bad that life expectancy had dropped by as much as 10 years for most people. In the industrial sector of Czechoslovakia, the air quality became so bad that individuals were given a bonus to work there, and the local residents called the bonus "burial money."

Government control does not equate to an improved environment, even when socialist nations make it a priority. North Korea uses 70 percent more energy for the same output as its South Korean counterpart. Before the fall of Communism, East Germany used 40 percent more energy per person than West Germany, yet it earned them a far lower standard of living. Less regulated governments and economies actually help to foster environmental stewardship, simply because they are responding to market forces, not government force.

■ GLOBAL COMMAND AND CONTROL

Command and control also proved to be disruptive to business as world trade grew throughout the past 25 years. The electronic age had fostered a virtual revolution in productivity, in efficient transportation, and most importantly, in satellite-linked communications that, for the first time, allowed companies to have immediate and direct control of far-flung operations.

Most companies chose to become global not by design, but as a competitive necessity. By 1983, fully 74 percent of all nonfood items sold in the United States crossed international borders to get to consumers. Increased competition in home markets meant companies would have to strive intensely for an ever-dwindling slice of the pie. To achieve the economies of scale necessary for profitability, it became essential to develop global products and expand the scope of sales across international borders.

Trading blocks became a way for companies to achieve essential economies of scale. The European Economic Community; the North American Free Trade Agreement; in South America, Mercosur and the Andean Pack; the Central American Common Market; and several new trading blocks in the Pacific Rim, have taken form. When the Soviet Union crumbled, its members recognized the necessity for economic interdependence. A core confederation formed around the Ukraine, Belorussia, and Russia, a potential trading block that was 290 million consumers strong.

Trading blocks had the potential to open trade, at least regionally, yet were unable to achieve their potential because of de facto trade barriers. The General Agreement on Tariffs and Trade (GATT) seemed powerless against these nontariff barriers—hundreds of rules and test procedures— which acted as effectively as any tariff to increase cost and constrain commerce.

Command and control, as practiced by individual nation states, became a way of using societal goals such as environmental quality and safety, to protect special home industries and markets. It was little more than thinly veiled protectionism. There seemed no way to navigate through this regulatory minefield. It became apparent that for each government, and each rule-making body within each government, to act as if it were the only rule-making body represented a needless waste of scarce resources, and posed a tremendous barrier to achieving global cooperation on environmental issues.

Over the past decade, industry has made efforts to take the lead and voluntarily police itself. A host of well-intentioned programs developed, including Global Environmental Management Initiatives (GEMI), Environmental Self Assessment Program, the International Chamber of Commerce's standards under its "Business Charter for Sustainable Development," and a wide range of corporate codes and practices. In addition, the Valdez Principles were formulated after the *Valdez* oil spill disaster. Investors and environmentalists joined together demanding environmental responsibility from domestic and international companies known as chronic polluters. All these efforts, however, failed to establish a viable, and most important, credible world consensus.

In a long series of United Nations-sponsored environmental conferences, the participants agreed that only worldwide standards would serve. The United Nations Environmental Program and the World Commission on

Environment and Development finally established a definitive group, under the leadership of Gro Harle Brundtland, prime minister of Norway. In 1988, this group published "Our Common Future," a document endorsing the need for a uniform, global environmental system. More than 50 world powers praised and endorsed the report.

Tangible progress finally came with the United Nations Earth Summit held in Rio de Janeiro, which brought business, government, and environmental leaders together in the largest ever environmental conference. At this 1992 meeting, attention was focused on the work being done with standards by an organization based in Geneva, Switzerland.

■ THE INTERNATIONAL ORGANIZATION FOR STANDARDIZATION

The International Organization for Standardization was the one organization that seemed to have the credibility, experience, and international support to initiate a voluntary global approach to environmental management. The I.S.O. had been around for a long time. Founded in 1946, I.S.O. was both an acronym and a homonym for "isos"—an ancient Greek word meaning "equal." The organization's goal was to establish an equal treatment when a set level of performance was required, or definable process or product were needed. Such criteria, once formally documented, become standards.

For the first 42 years of I.S.O.'s existence, the organization developed standards for particular products or equipment within individual global industries, from machine tools to CD players. The ISO standards defined procedures to measure, monitor, review, and revise these technologies. The ISO standard's goal, however, was broad. It set out to not only define technical standards but, in the words of I.S.O.'s charter, "develop cooperation in the spheres of intellectual, scientific, technological and economic activity." A sister organization also evolved in Geneva, the International Electrotechnical Commission (IEC), to develop standards for the electrical and new electronics industry. I.S.O. and IEC differed little in their approach, or in their commitment to support global cooperation.

As the global industrial world changed, I.S.O. leadership saw a need for a broader scope. As Lawrence Eicher, I.S.O. Secretary General, noted: "As our 10,000th standard illustrates, I.S.O.'s work has acquired new dimensions." The 10,000th standard was the ISO 11200 Series, which went beyond designating performance to setting a series of noise level standards that applied to all machinery.

I.S.O. reached world prominence after its 1987 publication of the first-ever total systems standards for quality assurance, ISO 9000. This internationally recognized quality management system provided criteria for achieving quality regardless of the size of an organization, where it was located, the type of product and service, or even its resources. The generic quality management system was applicable in virtually any situation. For major corporations around the world, ISO 9000 became the archetype for a systemic approach, and while not all companies sought ISO 9001 certification, the basic methods employed were almost universally embraced.

At the Earth Summit in 1992, I.S.O.'s success in quality management was already respected. And I.S.O. in cooperation with IEC had recently established a joint board on technical trends called SAGE (Strategic Advisory Group on the Environment), for the sole purpose of proposing a realistic global concept. SAGE was a major contributor in defining the outcome of Earth Summit. SAGE was central to a commitment to "sustainable development," which is an approach that uses the earth's resources "in a way that does not compromise the ability of future generations to meet their needs." From this came United Nations Agenda 21, a comprehensive set of 27 principles for achieving sustainable development. Together, they form a overriding philosophy of responsibility for our generation.

After the Earth Summit, things began happening rapidly. Great Britain was the first to recognize and adapt the ISO systems approach to environmental management. In March 1992, the British Standards Institution (BSI) created BS 7750, the first government-sponsored environmental rules that stressed overall environmental systems performance, rather than rigid line-item performance targets. Thousands of companies throughout Great Britain and the Americas took up BS 7750 as a better, more flexible way of coping with environmental responsibility. BS 7750, however, made routine audits mandatory, not voluntary. Regular audits were built into the approach to maintain certification status. While the concept was truly a step ahead, tough enforcement policies made it less attractive. Before BS 7750, a United Kingdom company that failed to meet an environmental standard was fined. Under BS 7750, noncompliance to regulations resulted in a loss of all contracts, and the company was out of business entirely. Eventually, this hard line was abandoned, and BS 7750 was re-released as voluntary standards.

The next idea in environmental management systems to cross the English Channel, when the European Union established its own version, was called the Eco-Management Audit Scheme (EMAS). Europe's strategy was to apply their standard to a hit list of 12,000 manufacturing sites that the European Union considered to be high-level polluters. This standard also required methodical audits, and a company's actual physical measures for control were made public, along with its continuous improvement goals.

By the end of 1995, most companies in Britain and Europe found they could not compete or do business without adopting either BS 7750 or EMAS certification. Lack of environmental commitment now came with a heavy price tag. Yet while innovative, the standards were still too narrowly focused on specific cultures to be universally accepted as the global solution.

Leadership came from I.S.O., which less than a year after the Earth Summit established Technical Committee 207 with the daunting responsibility to develop "standardization in the field of environmental management tools and systems." Technical committees were the traditional approach to ISO standards development. Committees with members from business, environmental, and government groups, representing more than 120 countries took part. ISO 14000 was drafted in record time.

Approval on both sides of the Atlantic was swift and decisive. The U.S. Technical Advisory Group (TAG), made up of several major U.S. standards groups, was so enthusiastic about ISO 14000 that they didn't wait for the standard's final approval before adopting ISO 14000 as America's national standard for an environmental management system. In Europe, endorsements came from most governments, including a suggestion that certification with ISO 14000 would automatically serve as EMAS certification. The need for a universal approach was so great, and respect for ISO 9000's success so complete, that ISO 14000 almost overnight became the world norm.

ISO 14000 found immediate acceptance with the global business community because it provided a reasoned solution and suggested a balance between environmental goals and the equally essential need for economic growth. There was no question that "richer is cleaner," that countries experiencing economic growth also fare better at assuming responsibility for the environment. Barriers to economic growth can impede environmental management. However, barriers in one country cause manufacturing facilities to move to countries where little, or few, barriers (i.e., environmental legislation or regulation) exist. Here, irresponsible companies can act with abandon, which consigns people living in these countries (usually Third World Nations) to conditions of growing environmental degradation, even while raising employment and wage rates.

For two generations, business had been saying "consider the costs": Every decision to address any environmental, social, or even political problem through the marketplace must come with a thorough understanding that there are costs involving capital, human resources, jobs, and effects on the standard of living. Sustainable environmental efforts, business contended, needed to go hand in hand with cost-efficiency. As U.S. President Bill Clinton said, "We need to focus on the things that matter, to expend our energies and resources where they can do the most good. That's the responsible way for any corner mom-and-pop store, and it should be the way we address our common need for a sustainable world environment."

Chapter 3

About ISO 14001

To have his path made clear for him is the aspiration of every human being in our beclouded and tempestuous existence.

—JOSEPH CONRAD

The evolution of ISO 9000 out of the British quality standard, BS 5750, was such that BS 5750 (the draft international standard) and ISO 9000 (as adopted) were virtually identical. Thus, companies that foresaw this turn of events were able to use BS 5750 as a template and, by adopting it, were both fully compliant and fully competitive the moment ISO 9000 went into effect.

This is *not* what happened with ISO 14000.

BS 7750, the British environmental management standard, is well geared for the United Kingdom and for the European Community as well (it was written to mesh with the

Community Eco-Management Scheme of 1994), but did not allow the flexibility needed by developing nations, Asian manufacturers, or the United States regarding regulatory compliance issues and management. While many aspects and core concepts of BS 7750 can be found in ISO 14000, the standard itself differs markedly.

Even the standard commonly referred to as "ISO 14000" throughout 1995 (one year prior to adoption) differs slightly from the standard as adopted. Prior to 1996, companies precertifying their environmental management systems to the standard were following "Draft International Standard ISO/DIS 14001." A later version, circulated in the latter part of that year, was known in draft form as "ISO/DIS 14001.2," and it was this draft that was eventually adopted as ISO 14001.

People used to the older version of the draft international standard, or those using books published prior to the actual adoption of the standard will find differences. For example, a reference to Section 4.3.6 (which dealt with Operational Control in ISO/DIS 14001) seems nonexistent in the actual standard, which only goes to Section 4.3.4, and then moves on to Section 4.4!

This is because the numbering system was changed between the earlier and later draft versions in Section 4. The section called "4.0" in ISO/DIS 14001 is called "4.1" in ISO/DIS 14001.2 (and in the final standard), thus all of Section 4 moves one subsection ahead in its numbering. With the two standards side by side, it's simple enough to compare them, but if you're only referring to numbers, it can be confusing.

In the next three chapters, the focus is on the actual Environmental Management Systems (EMS) section of the ISO 14000 standard, or ISO 14001. A full text of ISO 14001 (or, for all of ISO 14000) is available from the International

Organization for Standardization, Case Postale 56, CH-1211 Genève 20, Switzerland (alternately, many registrar organizations can also provide you with a copy of the current standard). You will find this document is essential if you're starting your EMS. This is the version of the standard that auditors reference when citing nonconformance or observations, so it's imperative to speak the same language.

For the convenience of those referring to the older draft—or those trying to make sense out of the preadoption reference texts—the *former* draft section numbers will appear in parentheses after the title of each subsection dealing with the mandatory elements of the specification in Chapter 5. You'll see these throughout Section 4 (the only section in which the numbering changed between drafts). These cross-references will allow you to follow along with either version of the standard.

■ THOU "SHALL . . . "

One of the first things to do as you read through the international standard is to take a highlighter pen and accentuate the word "shall" every time you see it (or, if your copy of the standard is on your computer, search for the word "shall" and italicize it, boldface it, or otherwise emphasize it).

Why? Because the term shall is the red flag of ISO 14001. Words have exact meanings in the standard, so shall (as opposed to "should") indicates a *mandatory* requirement. As an EMS manager, you must ensure that each shall so flagged is carried out—to the letter—or your EMS will be incomplete and, as a result, out of conformance with the standard.

There are 52 "shalls" in ISO 14001 as it was finally adopted, all of them in Section 4. Some are tightly focused, dot-the-"i" requirements; others are so broad and general in scope that they will affect every aspect of a company. By becoming aware of each mandatory requirement, you can craft an EMS that will meet the international standard and bring your company to ISO 14000 performance levels.

Just as important, once your EMS is up and running, the audits conducted on it will be run by auditors who are trained to look for adherence to each of these mandatory requirements. Auditors, as will be seen, have a considerable degree of freedom when it comes to running an audit. When it comes to mandatory requirements, though, that freedom narrows dramatically. Auditors *must* verify that each shall-flagged criterion exists within the EMS at hand. Developing this judgment is a critical part of their training, and it is also one of the touchstones that a registrar (a certifying organization—the firm that actually secures and employs the audit team) uses to evaluate auditor performance.

Take the shalls seriously, if for no other reason than your auditors will most definitely take them seriously. Every mandatory element must be present and met in your EMS. No other scenario is acceptable—51 out of 52 may bring you to 98 percent, but it is *not* a passing grade as far as ISO 14000 is concerned.

■ FAMILIAR TERRITORY

If you have ever implemented or worked with ISO 9001— the management-system portion of ISO 9000, the international standard for quality—you will recognize some familiar management-system principles as you go through ISO 14001 (the similarity in the "-001" suffixes of the two standards is entirely intentional).

Like ISO 9000, the ISO 14000 standard's language is generic: It can be applied to any organization, of any type, size, or complexity, anywhere in the world. And like ISO 9000, ISO 14000 has documentation requirements that assure consistency and clarity, and that form the backbone of an evolving and repeatable management system.

The two standards differ in terms of the publics affected by them. ISO 9000, being a quality standard, mainly affects a company's customers (although, in the long run, it also affects the company itself, as repeat business is closely linked to consistent quality). Since ISO 14000 is an environmental standard, the publics affected by it are virtually infinite—from the worker on the plant floor to the person 500 miles downwind of a plant's emissions to the county officials who may have to deal with remediation issues decades after a plant has closed.

Management—and front-line—personnel need to be trained in the intent of ISO 14000. ISO 14000 is a management system that empowers employees and impacts performance level. Management sets the policies that guide and facilitate changes by those front-line operators. Figure 3-1 illustrates the matrix for ISO 14000 training.

Not surprisingly, the aims of ISO 9000 and ISO 14000 standards mesh nicely; for example, a company that reduces or eliminates "rejects" from its output also reduces or eliminates the energy and/or waste issues of recycling or disposal of those subquality parts. Thus, improved quality results in improved environmental management.

The standards also mesh nicely in methodology, and a company already running to ISO 9000 standards will find the way smooth for implementing ISO 14000.

But, just as ISO 9000 is not an "instruction book" on achieving quality, neither is ISO 14000 a how-to on environmental control. ISO 9000-certified companies reach their own definitions of quality and improvement, and use the standard as a means of realizing those definitions. Similarly,

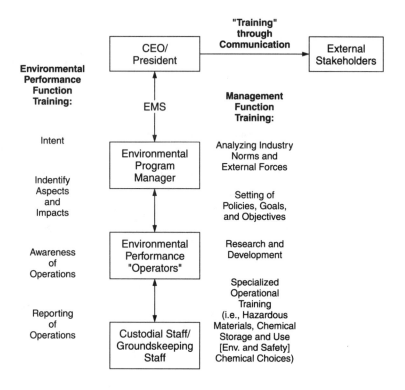

Figure 3-1. ISO 14000 Training Matrix

ISO 14000 will not tell you *how* to be environmentally responsible. Your organization's top management (guided by forces from external sources including existing and upcoming government or industry regulations, societal issues, and technological developments) will use the standard as a road map. This road map will help you arrive at your company's self-defined image of environmental responsibility.

■ DOCUMENTATION

Peruse ISO 14001, and the first thing you are likely to notice will be the standard's requirements for documentation.

The business that runs without documentation must depend on verbal communications for its records, adherence to procedures, and understanding of goals and statement of policies. Such a business will face great risks and may not run very long at all.

If any management system is to work, documentation is essential. Even in the smallest of companies, things need to be documented and kept where they can be found.

Information has to be recorded *and* available to the people who need it. It is practical and laudable to have a 10-step procedure for safely disposing of the waste lubricating oil from a metal band saw—but the procedure does no good if the saw operator has never seen or heard of it.

ISO 14001, then, takes a thorough approach for documentation and communication of this documentation. The standard requires you to record your company's environmental management policy, to set down the procedures for realizing (and for measurement of your success in realizing) that policy, to deliver instructions to those who must implement the procedures, and to keep score on how well those instructions were carried out.

As noted in the preceding paragraph, there are *four* primary documentation requirements in ISO 14001. Here they are again, with some comment on how to apply them in your company:

➤ *Environmental policy statements.* These must originate from the company's top management. Policy statements summarize how your company plans to meet the requirements of ISO 14000. Policy statements can be recorded in an Environmental Management System manual, but such a manual is not required. There are other ways of recording environmental policies. If your company has implemented IS0 9000, you probably already have a Quality Management System Manual into which you could easily fold your EMS policies (yet another reason for certifying your organization to both standards).

➤ *Standard operating procedures.* If you're a manager, you're probably intimately familiar with the "SOPs" of business. Standard operating procedures are to a management system what dual-entry ledgers are to an accounting system. Try to run a business without them, and you'll soon find yourself with no business to run.

The best companies have standard operating procedures for everything, from starting a shift to putting out a fire. The SOP describes what is to be done, when and where it is to be done and by whom, and how it is to be done. These procedures are generally collected in a procedural manual.

Environmental Management Procedures can be kept in their own manual, but to keep them from being overlooked, it is more effective overall to include them in a manual along with your company's other procedures. There should be procedures both for normal operations (recycling workers' plant apparel) and for emergencies (dealing with an oil spill). Far-reaching and detailed thinking in the creation of these procedural records can go a long way in preparing your company for a wide variety of contingencies, as well as taking the guesswork out of everyday duties.

➤ *Job instructions.* Unlike ISO 9000, ISO 14000 does not require separate job instructions. Job instructions tell individuals and small teams how to perform specific tasks. Job instructions pertinent to your EMS may be part of a detailed procedure. This detailed procedure must tell your people how to perform tasks in the most consistent, energy-efficient, and environmentally controlled manner possible. These procedures must be deployed throughout a company and either kept on hand, or displayed where work is performed. Procedures should reference all guidelines used by the worker, such as good laboratory practices or EPA report forms.

➤ *Records.* "Keeping score" means that you must quantify and record the outcomes of procedures or work performed. Your organization doubtlessly keeps procedural or work records already. Specific examples of records will be flagged in the discussion of ISO 14001, element by element.

Documentation is critical to satisfying ISO 14000 (as well as ISO 9000). It is objective evidence that provides certainty that your company is performing to these standards.

Chapter 4

Scope and Definitions

Without words to objectify and characterize our sensations and place them in relation to one another, we cannot evolve a tradition of what is real in the world.

—Ruth Hubbard

This chapter presents a commentary on the ISO 14001 EMS standard, with some quotations from the standard to illustrate or illuminate an element. Be certain that, in addition to reading about ISO 14001, you take the time to thoroughly familiarize yourself with the standard itself.

The following sections will provide a look at the various elements of "ISO 14001—Environmental Management Systems—specification with guidance for use."

1 SCOPE

This part of the Specification looks briefly at what ISO 14001 does and does not do (i.e., it gives the reader the requirements for an environmental management system (EMS), but it does not state what the specific environmental-outcome goals of that EMS should be). The opening paragraph of this element says that the Specification allows an organization to *"formulate a policy and objectives"* in light of *"legislative requirements and information about significant environmental impacts."* An EMS is reasonably expected to apply to subjective matters—*"those environmental aspects which the organization can control and over which it can be expected to have an influence."*

What organizations can use ISO 14000? Section 1 of ISO 14001 lists five qualifiers, stating that it is applicable to *"any organization that wishes to:"*

1a *implement, maintain and improve an environmental management system;*

"Improve" here can be taken in two ways. One is that the ISO 14001 Specification can be used to either start a new EMS or bring an old one into conformance with the standard. The other is that continual and ongoing improvement is an integral part of the standard.

1b *assure itself of its conformance with its stated environmental policy;*

Self-assurance is important because, as evident in "1e," self-determination and self-declaration are a part of the standard.

1c *demonstrate such conformance to others;*

Estimates vary, but a large part of the move toward ISO 14000 certification will likely be driven by company-to-vendor mandates from larger corporations; for many companies, ISO 14000 certification will become part of the "price of admission" for doing business with the major participants in many industries.

1d *seek certification/registration of its environmental management system by an external organization;*

This certification and registration is not done by the International Organization for Standardization, but by companies known as "registrars"—which themselves are certified by another organization one step removed from ISO. These registrars conduct audits of a company's EMS, but their inspections of a company's operation do not, in and of themselves, guarantee conformance to the international standard. Auditors seek evidence of a system's adequacy, effectiveness, and conformance. Auditors identify nonconformances and problem areas that exist during the time the audit is conducted, and in the areas that the auditors choose to examine. Just as a driver's-license exam tests the applicant's knowledge on selected questions, instead of making the person recite the entire motor-vehicle code, an EMS audit assays an organization's performance by looking at bits and pieces of the system, rather than by dissecting the entire system in exhaustive detail.

1e *make a self-determination and self-declaration of conformance with this international standard.*

Your organization is responsible for deciding whether it is in conformance with the standard. The registrar, and its audit team, merely look at selected parts of your system to verify that this is so. To use the driver's-license analogy, the license exam merely determines whether the applicant knows how to operate a motor vehicle safely and legally—it is the new driver's responsibility to then use that knowledge and drive within the parameters of the law. An EMS is what social scientists call a "living" process; it goes on operating day to day, not just on the day in which it is audited, and the audit process does not "close the loop" on the system. For an EMS to work, it must be embraced by everyone at every level within an organization, and it must become an integral part of an organization's culture.

2 NORMATIVE REFERENCES

Normative references, in ISO nomenclature, are other pertinent international standards (in this case, environmental-management-related) that the authors of the Specification feel would be useful for an organization to employ in meeting the requirements. This is the easiest section of the ISO 14001 Specification to deal with since, as initially adopted, ISO 14001 made no normative references whatsoever; skip this part and go on.

3 DEFINITIONS

Just as ISO 14000 helps ensure that everyone is "reading from the same book" when it comes to environmental management systems, Section 3 helps ensure that all involved are "speaking the same language" when discussing the key points of the international standard.

You may be tempted to skip or skim the definitions and get on to Section 4, which itemizes the essential do's and don'ts of the Specification. But I strongly suggest that you resist that temptation. Many of the words and phrases in ISO 14000 have narrower or more specialized meanings than the definitions you'll find in the average dictionary or currently used within industry. The purpose of this definition section is to clarify exactly what the Specification means when a particular word or phrase is used, before you begin attempting to implement the standard.

Speaking of definitions, this book often uses the terms, "section" or "subsection" to refer to a part of the international Specification. Technically, this is incorrect—the units that make up each clause (section) are referred to as "elements" or "subclauses." But North Americans tend to use the more familiar "section," and "element" tends to confuse people, particularly in an environmental sense (to a North American, carbon and oxygen are elements . . .). Therefore, this book substitutes the more familiar terminology.

That little departure won't matter much. But others will. Because the Specification definitions have exact meanings, each definition is listed here verbatim—as it appears in the Specification. Comments draw attention to the special implications contained within each definition.

3.1 *Continual improvement*

process of enhancing the environmental management system to achieve improvements in overall environmental performance in line with the organization's environmental policy

NOTE—The process need not take place in all areas of activity simultaneously

Although the two phrases may be used interchangeably in everyday conversation, there is a subtle, but important, difference between "continual improvement" and "continuous improvement," as they pertain to the standard. "Continual" means "frequent and regular." "Continuous" means "without breaks or interruptions." A dotted line is continual and a solid line is continuous. If your wastewater quality monitoring shows improvements on a weekly, monthly, or quarterly basis, then you have effected a continual improvement. On the other hand, to effect a *continuous* improvement, you will have to demonstrate that the water quality gets better from one moment to the next—an impossible task (even if it could be done, it would quickly reach a point at which it could not be measured), and one for which the documentation costs would be enormous, to say the least.

Clause 4 of ISO 14001 is geared toward a process of *continual* (not continuous) improvement. It goes by the numbers: Section 4.1 guides you in the determination of an environmental policy; Section 4.2 addresses how you plan to realize that policy; Section 4.3 deals with methods of implementing the plans; Section 4.4 gives the Specification's requirements for measuring, monitoring, and (where necessary) correcting; and Section 4.5 specifies the need for management review—which in turn will result in more planning, and so on in a continual (not continuous) cycle.

ISO has appended a note to this definition that has decided cost implications. Let's say that you have decided over the next 10 years to reduce your manufacturing facility's air emission levels, noise levels, landfill use, and wastewater output. Assuming that all four of these are in, and will remain within, compliance with all applicable laws and government standards, there is no imperative within ISO 14000 for you to attack all four fronts simultaneously. Nor may you want to—the human resources and out-of-pocket costs may be more than what is economically feasible for your organization. Air scrubbers, for example, are enormously expensive to install and upgrade; during the fiscal year when you do that, you may not make any progress on further reducing noise levels—and that's okay, as long as you specify it in your environmental management plan or records of management review.

3.2 *Environment*

surroundings in which an organization operates, including air, water, land, natural resources, flora, fauna, humans, and their interrelation

NOTE—Surroundings in this context extend from within an organization to the global system

We tend to think of the environment as natural entities such as the rain forests or the oceans. These are all part of the environment in general, and may very well be part of the environment as it pertains to your organization. But so is the booth where your workers are painting your products. So is the neighboring farmer. So is the lake, 600 miles and two countries away, that is impacted by your exhaust stack emissions.

If something could, no matter how remotely, be impacted by your existence and activities, it is considered part of the environment as defined by Section 3 of the Specification. Tall buildings may have an effect on the wind immediately around them—they don't add pollution to it, or fill it with grit, or discolor it, but they can accelerate it, block it, or change its direction. Is wind a part of the environment? You bet it is. And if your community's trees are adversely affected by winds generated by your building, the community has a legitimate environmental complaint against you.

"Environment," as defined here, does not have the lakes-and-wilderness connotation which it is so often granted in casual use. The inside of your plant is an environment, the places where your products are used are environments, and the earth, land, water, animals, and people around your facilities is an environment. Think in wide-reaching, global terms.

3.3 *Environmental aspect*

> element of an organization's activities, products or services that can interact with the environment
>
> *NOTE*—A significant environmental aspect is an environmental aspect that has or can have a significant environmental impact.

Here's another nuance of which you should take special note; the word "can" in this instance indicates that you should be aware of *potential* interaction with the environment, as well as actual interaction. Oil in a sealed container may have no interaction with the environment around it, but if the container leaks, the interaction could be far-reaching and significant (e.g., *Valdez*). Furthermore, significant may not mean regulated (e.g., significant or high use of electrical energy).

3.4 *Environmental impact*

> any change to the environment, whether adverse or beneficial, wholly or partially resulting from an organization's activities, products or services

There is a natural tendency to think of "environmental impact" in a negative sense, just as there is a natural tendency to think of "environmental management" in terms of reduction of pollution, waste, or resource usage.

Actually—as this definition shows—the converse is also true. There are such things as positive environmental impacts, and it is strongly suggested that you strive for them. Positive environmental impacts provide strong public relations. This will lift your company's image as a good corporate citizen. Wetlands restoration, community forestry programs, discharge of wastewater that is *cleaner* than your intake source, and company participation in highway, river, or public park cleanups in support of nonprofit organizations are all examples of how your organization can have a positive environmental impact and gain community support.

Another reason to include varied positive environmental impacts is that the things one party considers positive could be considered negative by another. If you landscape your storm retention pond for wildlife it may be considered a positive impact by hunters and bird lovers who are lobbying for increased waterfowl habitat; but it could be considered a negative by the neighbors who will get goose droppings on their lawns, or have to deal with mosquitoes hatched out of your pond. Such "lateral thinking" will help you evaluate the ramifications of your organization's operations and plans.

3.5 *Environmental management system*

> the part of the overall management system that includes organizational structure, planning activities, responsibilities, practices, procedures, processes and resources for developing, implementing, achieving, reviewing and maintaining the environmental activity

This definition changed significantly from that used in the draft international standard circa 1995 (ISO/DIS 14001). One of the most prominent differences is the opening phrase, "the part of the overall management system. . . . "

One of the prime requisites of a good environmental management system is a buy-in by the top management of a company. Another is integration of sound environmental thinking into the planning and operation of all company activities. Neither is likely to happen if the EMS is separate from the overall management system.

The Specification definition of an EMS implies top management direction and participation, and makes environmental management what it should be—a day-to-day function of the organization.

3.6 *Environmental management system audit*

a systematic and documented verification process of objectively obtaining and evaluating evidence to determine whether an organization's environmental management system conforms to the environmental management system audit criteria set by the organization, and for communication of this process to management

Again, conventional wisdom aside, an audit does not certify that you're doing everything right. It merely certifies that what it examined (a scope determined by the audit team and its client) was free of nonconformances to the standard at the time the examination was made.

The organization is supposed to monitor its own activities. The audit also determines whether an organization's EMS is adequate and if the resources needed for operation of the EMS have been provided.

Note that the audit is performed against your organization's own criteria (i.e., policies, procedures, and ISO 14001: 1996). The audit team has the option to determine if those criteria are appropriate and adequate for the organization at hand, and it has an obligation to cite as nonconformances any practices that violate prevailing environmental laws or government regulations. This citation does not mean failure to meet legal compliance, per se, but failure to identify legal requirements or to operate in defiance of such knowledge. Other than that, your organization is free to determine the size and type of its environmental playing field.

3.7 *Environmental objective*

> overall environmental goal, arising from the environmental policy, that an organization sets itself to achieve, and which is quantified where practicable

This—the what-are-we-going-to-do part of environmental management—is easier to put into practice if you follow the advice implicit in this definition, and quantify your desired outcomes.

This quantification can be a combination of a measured number and a time span ("We will reduce solid waste from all of our facilities by 50 percent over the next five years"), or it can be purely chronological ("We will meet all emissions standards of the 19XX Clean Air regulation three years before it comes into force"). Either way, it gives your organization a finish line—for this lap, at least—that it can see and strive for. It also provides auditors with objective evidence by which they can measure the effectiveness of the EMS.

3.8 *Environmental performance*

> measurable results of the environmental management system, related to an organization's control of its environmental aspects, based on its environmental policy, objectives and targets

"When you announce measure, measure what you are speaking about, and express it in numbers, you know something about it . . . ."

That's how William Thomson, Lord Kelvin (the inventor of the degree-of-brightness scale used for measuring lights) underlines the importance of measurement.

Objective evidence of environmental performance must be expressed as numbers, which are the result of the measurement of that performance. This is important, because it lets you know up front that measurement (and documentation of that measurement) is a prerequisite for proving that your organization is moving toward or reaching its environmental goals.

3.9 *Environmental policy*

statement by the organization of its intentions and principles in relation to its overall environmental performance which provides a framework for action and for the setting of its environmental objectives and targets

Two words missing from this definition that are (or should be) universally understood are "clear and concise." Your environmental policy is a statement—usually no more than a few paragraphs long—summarizing how you approach environmental issues, who approves and supports it (top management), how the policy is appropriate for the organization at hand, and what your organization is committed to; it should also affirm that you are committed to continual improvement (see definition 3.1). Auditors will measure the clarity and conciseness of your company's policy.

3.10 *Environmental target*

detailed performance requirement, quantified where practicable, applicable to the organization of parts or parts thereof, that arises from the environmental objectives and needs to be set and met in order to achieve those objectives

An environmental target might be "to conserve energy by reducing, between January 1, 1999, and December 31, 1999, the amount of electricity used at all company facilities by 25 percent, as measured in terms of kilowatts hours consumed per unit of product, compared with 1998 levels."

This statement explains, in detail, what objective is being met ("to conserve energy"), how the organization intends to meet it ("by reducing . . . the amount of electricity used at all company facilities"), and quantifies the target in terms of amount ("by 25 percent"), time ("between January 1, 1999, and December 31, 1999"), unit of measurement used ("as measured in terms of kilowatt hours consumed per unit of product"), and the baseline for measurement ("compared with 1998 levels").

Anyone with access to the organization's 1998 and 1999 production records and electricity usage records should be able to calculate the indicators and determine whether this target has been met. That is as it should be: Targets should be black-and-white, easily determined goals; quantification helps to demonstrate whether or not those goals have been met.

3.11 *Interested party*

individual or group concerned with or affected by the environmental performance of an organization

The language, "concerned with or affected by," opens this part of the Specification up considerably. The latter portion, "affected by . . . " refers to a neighbor downwind of your smelter, a person whose well shares the same aquifer as your freshwater intake, or even the fellow whose view of the sunrise will be blocked by your new manufacturing facility. But it also refers to a resident of a state in which your internal-combustion-engine-powered product will be operated, or someone in a country faced with the task of disposing of your product or packaging after purchase and use. Someone "affected by" the environmental performance of your organization could be virtually *anyone.*

This is one extremely important difference between ISO 9000 and ISO 14000. Your "quality public"—those individuals or groups affected by your quality performance"—is mostly limited to your customers and the customers of your customers. But your "environmental public" is widespread, and may well be global.

And to make this definition even more broad-ranging, the authors of ISO 14001 also use the phrase "concerned with." If someone *shows* interest, that person is an interested party.

Are your customers interested parties? Of course they are. Your neighbors? Absolutely. Government agencies? It goes without saying. Workers and unions working in your shop? You bet. Investors and shareholders? Yes, indeed.

And so are environmental activist groups, civic organizations, social and welfare organizations, political alliances— you name it. If they raise their hand, they're interested.

At first, this might seem alarming. However, you are not giving everyone free rein to examine your organization's activities. With ISO 14000, you communicate your environmental policy, and any additional information you choose to the public. Public availability of the policy is a requirement of the standard, which will be discussed later in this book.

The upside is that certification to the ISO 14000 standard is a *voluntary* and *proactive* measure, taken by your organization above and beyond those steps required by regulation. That feature speaks for itself: ISO 14000-oriented companies choose to step forward and so automatically assume the environmental responsibility characteristics of forward-thinking companies. If you set up your system properly, those who look at your company through the portals of ISO 14000 will evaluate you as the responsible and methodical, environmentally conscious organization that the standard was designed to encourage. Don't fear the "interested parties."

3.12 *Organization*

company, corporation, firm, enterprise, authority or institution, in part or combination thereof, whether incorporated or not, public or private, that has its own functions and administration

NOTE—For organizations with more than one operating unit, a single operating unit may be defined as an organization

As here defined, an "organization" can be an international mega-corporation with more than 100 plants in countries all over the world, or it can be the welding shop owned by the subsidiary of that megacorporation. You may choose (possibly because of vendor requirements in a contract you've recently won) to certify only one of your facilities. That is fine, as long as the facility falls within the stated definition (*" . . . its own functions and administration"*).

Some entities generally known as "organizations" will not qualify as such under this definition—industry alliances, informal joint ventures, and so on—if they do not have one central, top management to which they must ultimately report. For an entity to be an organization under ISO 14000, there must be a responsible party who has the authority to approve of, disapprove of, or mandate change within the management system.

3.13 *Prevention of pollution*

use of processes, practices, materials or products that avoid, reduce or control pollution, which may include recycling, treatment, process changes, control mechanisms, efficient use of resources and material substitution

NOTE—the potential benefits of prevention of pollution include the reduction of adverse environmental impacts, improved efficiency and reduced costs

In the 1960s, public concern over pesticides in foods rose to such a height that legislation was eventually passed requiring no detectable levels whatsoever of certain pesticide agents in foodstuffs. By 1996, these laws had to be revised—not because public standards of purity had lessened, but because measurement technology had become so sophisticated that previously acceptable foods were now failing to meet the standards.

This is just one example of why "never say never" is generally a good adage to follow. And in this spirit, "prevention of pollution," as defined in this Specification, does not mean "the elimination of any possibility of pollution."

Rather, the Specification allows that efforts to "avoid, reduce or control pollution" are acceptable as pollution-prevention initiatives. In the production of goods demanded and needed by the public, pollution prevention may be impossible.

The authors of ISO 14001 recognize that most groups using the standard are businesses, and that businesses have the fiduciary responsibility to turn a profit. In the added Note, they further recognize that many pollution-prevention initiatives can reduce overhead and help contribute to greater profits. While pollution prevention may not be possible, it can be regarded as ideal, and pollution minimization is a target within reach in most issues.

From another perspective, the standard also calls for continual improvement, a better bit-by-bit method of ameliorating negative situations and creating positive ones. Within this philosophy, zero pollution is not the immediate goal. The goal is a methodical march closer toward zero.

The Specification speaks of "processes, practices, materials or products"—four roads to pollution prevention. In paint technology, the use of water-based paints is a process that can prevent pollution. Recovering and recycling excess pigment powder is a practice which can prevent pollution. The powder-coat finish (which has little or no solvent) is a material that can prevent pollution. And the less toxic substances that are substituted for heavy metals in paints are products that prevent pollution. All of these have been widely used by the major auto companies to reduce their plant emissions and lower the waste produced by paint lines.

Chapter 5

ISO 14001

Clause (Section) 4

Synergy means behavior of whole systems unpredicted by the behavior of their parts.

—R. BUCKMINSTER FULLER

The essential core of ISO 14001 is Section 4. Again, it is this section that contains all the "shalls" referred to earlier: Section 4 is the EMS manager's bible. Follow it closely, and you will have a system that satisfies the international standard and integrates sound environmental thinking into every aspect of your company and allows prediction of performance outcomes.

As noted earlier, the numbers in parentheses refer to the sections of the Specification as they were numbered in the 1995 Draft International Standard.

Figure 5-1 illustrates the implementation cycle for ISO 14001. The illustration serves two purposes. First, it graphically demonstrates the grouping of the elements. Second, it demonstrates the principle of continual improvement that is so vital to ISO 14000. Because you are constantly evaluating and making changes to your EMS, the practice of continual improvement is inherent in the implementation process.

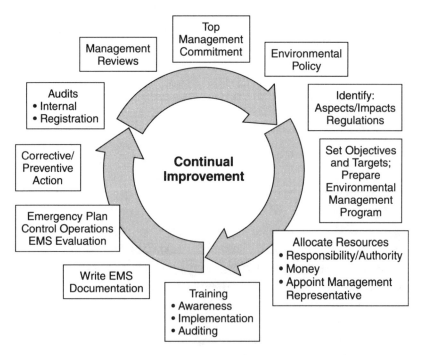

Figure 5-1. ISO 14001 Implementation Cycle

4 ENVIRONMENTAL MANAGEMENT SYSTEM REQUIREMENTS

4.1 *General requirements (4.0)*

The first mandatory requirement appears here. This part of the Specification reads, *"The organization* shall *establish and maintain an environmental management system. . . . "* Note that there are two verbs in this sentence: *establish* and *maintain.* You cannot simply set up an EMS and then leave it while you go on to a new task. The EMS must become part of the daily fabric of the organization.

The word, "maintain," in these criteria almost always implies a need for up-to-date documentation, so look for it, as well as "shall," when reading the Specification. This clues you in on the written evidence that will be required when your organization undergoes an environmental management system audit.

Section 4.1 of the ISO 14001 Specification directs companies that desire ISO 14000 certification not only to put an EMS in place, but to take steps to keep the EMS running at a level which will satisfy all requirements of the standard. This section then goes on to explain that the requirements of an EMS are explained in detail in the whole of Clause 4 (Sections 4.1 through 4.5).

4.2 *Environmental policy (4.1)*

A second mandatory element of the Specification appears here:

Top management *shall* define the organization's environmental policy. . . .

Why top management? Two reasons, really.

One is that only the organization's upper echelon of management will have the scope—the width or range of vision—to define a policy that adequately covers all of an organization's activities. Lower managers generally are accountable for only a portion of an organization's activities, and so will tend to compartmentalize and concentrate the EMS on those segments of the organization with which they are most familiar.

Another reason for mandating top management involvement is that objects dropped from high places tend to have more impact. The members of the Technical Advisory Groups (TAGs) that helped create ISO 14000 are almost all people from the business world; they know how things work within corporations. They recognize that a program advanced by a manager's subordinate (or his or her peer) may be given short shrift or even ignored, whereas a policy set down by a CEO or the equivalent will get everyone's fullest attention.

Top management involvement means that the environmental policy cannot be ignored, and that those who neglect it are always answerable to a higher authority. This structure fosters the longevity of the EMS, and safeguards it from abandonment when transient situations (a drop in dividends, shifts in market share, etc.) divert workers' and middle managers' attentions elsewhere.

The third issue is that those who control the mandates for the system must also control allocation of resources.

The second *"shall"* then continues by listing those things that top management *must* ensure concerning an organization's environmental policy:

> **4.2a** ... *appropriate to the nature, scale and environmental impacts of its activities, products or services.*

Let's say you have a multinational company that manufactures outboard motors for boats and other small watercraft. These motors are used on all manner of lakes, rivers, and nearshore ocean areas, and are predominantly powered by two-stroke internal combustion engines (lubricating oil is mixed with the fuel and consumed as part of the combustion process). The motors are made in a plant with the usual manufacturing capacities (metal milling, forging, paint application, etc.) and are shipped in containers of sufficient size to protect the product.

In this scenario, your products alone have a potential for environmental impact all over the globe. How much petroleum fuel (a limited resource) does the product use? What is the content of the exhaust emissions? Most outboards emit their exhaust underwater: Does this mean that unburned fuel and lubricants can be left there? What about noise? And how about disposal of the motor after it has come to the end of its life cycle?

How much energy must be used to ship the product from the plants to the wholesaler or dealer? What becomes of the shipping container? How much paper (another resource) is used in the documentation that must accompany the product?

What kinds of emissions do the plants produce and discharge into the environment? What happens to used lubricating oils from milling machines, overspray from paint lines, rejected parts produced by out-of-specification fabricators? How much electricity, natural gas, and water does the manufacturing process consume? What becomes of the wastewater?

Are the plants noisy? Does any part of the manufacturing process generate irritating gases or objectionable odors? How well are the facilities integrated into their surroundings?

What about suppliers? Where are they located and how far must they ship parts to the plants? What sorts of resources are expended in packaging supplier-to-plant shipments? Do suppliers have an EMS in place or plans to implement one?

How far must workers commute to their jobs? Are they all driving their own cars, or is carpooling or public transportation available?

Does the lunch hour require that employees go elsewhere (burning fuel to do so) or is attractive on-site dining available?

When you look at all the environmental ramifications implicit in such a company—from the effects of the workers' commute to the effect the product has on the environment—it becomes obvious that the *nature* and *scale* of the operation and its products are wide, and the potential *environmental impacts* are considerable.

In this case, the job is simply not going to get done by a policy that resolves merely to recycle the toner cartridges from the laser printer and turn the office wastepaper into memo pads. The environmental policy needs to reflect the realities of the situation to meet the intent of ISO 14001.

If you are looking at an organization within an organization (say, the manufacturing division of a large industrial corporation), the policy of the smaller entity must fit well and work within the policy of the larger one. Communication is critical to success.

Implicit in this process is the need for input from every area of the organization, to provide top management with the information to craft a workable environmental policy or to review its operations. In reality, this input will usually come to a task force, which will assemble the background and draft executive summaries—and probably even draft versions of the policy itself—to be used by top management in defining and evaluating the system, its requirements, and its documentation.

> **4.2b** *. . . commitment to continual improvement and prevention of pollution . . .*

As noted in the discussion of Section 3 (Definitions), this is not the Herculean task it first appears to be. *"Continual improvement"* can be improvement by stages, or improvement in regular, incremental steps over a period of time. *"Prevention of pollution"* can be reduction or minimization of pollution, as opposed to the sudden and absolute cessation of waste, noise, unsightliness, emissions to air or water, and so forth.

In other words, management here ensures that the organization will remain sustainable while improving its environmental posture and preventing pollution as required by the standard.

Gradual improvements are not only simpler to accomplish; they also contribute to the acceptance of an environmental management system and its accompanying goals.

If, for example, you plan to install a wastewater treatment facility that will make your plant's discharge water 75 percent cleaner, there is nothing in the Specification or the standard that requires you to make that 75 percent improvement your initial target; for one thing, what if it doesn't perform as expected as soon as it is installed? You might immediately find yourself behind schedule.

If, on the other hand, you take a reasonable portion of that expected improvement, and make *it* one of your first-year targets, you will have a goal that is reachable and realistic, and that allows you to fulfill standard requirements in a manner without unduly disrupting your day-to-day business. That 75 percent improvement can be divided into five annual segments of 15 percent and you can take credit for each incremental improvement in its turn, even if you are able to hit the 75 percent level in your very first year. ISO 14000 is designed to encourage you to improve your environmental standing, not to require you to perform miracles.

> **4.2c** . . . *commitment to comply with relevant environmental legislation and regulations, and with other requirements* . . .

Your environmental management system is not going to be acceptable if you deliberately break (and continue to break) the law regarding emissions, waste disposal, recycling requirements, noise or light pollution, and the like. Sometimes industry, trade association, contractual, or other targets will go above and beyond what the law requires, and these commitments, too, must be met.

The purpose of Section 4.2c is to set a baseline requirement that—because of the wide range of countries and industries across which ISO 14000 must function—the standard, and the ISO 14001 Specification cannot set by itself.

The standard calls for a *"commitment to comply,"* rather than "compliance." Ongoing legal non-compliance has to be rectified as the EMS is put in place. This language recognizes that, and further implies that demonstrated intent to put your organization in compliance with every environmental standard affecting it satisfies conformance to the standard. But recognize that "commitment" is far stronger than "intent to" or "involvement with."

> **4.2d** . . . *framework for setting and reviewing environmental targets and objectives* . . .

A "target" is a *"detailed performance requirement,"* whereas an objective is an *"overall environmental goal"*; you can think of the target as a detailed portion of the objective.

As shown in the example under 4.2a, a company's objectives and targets can be varied and far-reaching, pertaining not only to the company's own facilities, but to its products, its services, and its interaction with its suppliers and the communities within which it operates. In addition, most organizations are dynamic; they are in a constant state of change, forever creating new fronts that must be considered as management looks at its overall environmental picture.

These forces create a need for regular review of exactly what it is that the organization is trying to accomplish with its environmental policy. New areas of business may create new environmental needs. New technologies may open new environmental opportunities. It is easy for a plan to slip out-of-date in as little as a year, so continual monitoring and review, a requirement of ISO 14001, will prove to be a wise and—in the end—time-saving policy.

> **4.2e** *. . . documented, maintained and communicated to all employees . . .*

The word, "maintain" in Section 4.2 of the draft standard, implied that documentation would be required. In the final standard, the documentation requirement is set down in black and white. Top management is responsible for seeing that the organization's environmental policy is documented and kept current, and that every single employee—from the CEO to the newest hire—understands it and embraces it.

A general memo may seem like the way to go, but be honest—do *you* read every blanket memo that comes across your desk? Likewise, the group meeting will only be partially effective, as it misses those people who are off-site, ill, on vacation, or otherwise absent the day of the meeting, and it also misses those individuals who hire in after the familiarization meeting.

If you have the resources, using varied media (posters, newsletters, videotapes, e-mail, etc.) is arguably the best way to communicate your policy to employees. Signed affidavits help verify that this process is taking place and that every employee is aware of the environmental policy.

But the actions of management speak louder than words. Show employees that management believes in the policy and all operations will meet the policy's criteria.

4.2f . . . *available to the public.*

At first glance, keeping a stock of printed environmental-policy pamphlets on hand, and mailing them out to parties that ask for them, might seem like the best way to satisfy this requirement. Certainly, you will need to have some sort of a system in place to answer requests for the policy.

But don't stop there. A much more proactive stance is desirable. Even though having a quality management system (QMS) in place can make implementing an environmental management system both simpler and less expensive, you will still have invested considerable time, money, and effort into setting up your EMS, and it only stands to reason that you should reap the public-relations and marketing benefits of that endeavor.

The details of marketing your environmental commitment are covered in Chapter 11, but for starters, printing the policy on customer materials sent out with your products, including it with quotes or invoices, and similarly packaging it with your everyday customer correspondence can make great strides in communicating your policy and position regarding environmental responsibility to what is arguably your most *important* public—the customers who are already dealing with you.

4.3 *Planning (4.2)*

It is a rare endeavor, indeed, that is not made better by careful reflection and planning. In ISO 14000, planning is mandatory. Of the 52 mandatory elements contained in ISO 14001, 10 are contained in this, the Planning section of the Specification.

4.3.1 *Environmental aspects (4.2.1)*

The third, fourth, and fifth "shalls" of ISO 14001 are found in Section 4.3.1.

The first specifies that organizations must *"establish and maintain (a) procedure(s) to identify . . . environmental aspects . . . over which it can be expected to have an influence. . . . "*

"Environmental aspects," again, are elements of your *"activities, products or services which can interact with the environment."* These can be anything from the packaging containing your fast-food product to the lights in the parking lot at your manufacturing facility. It is management's responsibility to establish which of these aspects can have a significant impact on the environment.

There are six basic areas to consider when identifying environmental aspects:

1. Emissions to air.

2. Releases to water.

3. Waste management.

4. Contamination or degredation of land.

5. Use of basic materials and natural resources.

6. Local environmental and community issues.

Consideration should be given not only to normal operating conditions, but to startups, shutdowns, changes in operations, and foreseeable emergency conditions. For example, if constructing a new facility, soil erosion on site (degradation) is an aspect.

The fourth "shall" requires the organization to ensure that these aspects " . . . *are considered in setting its environmental objectives.* "

We saw in Section 4.2a that an organization's environmental policy must be " . . . *appropriate to the nature, scale and environmental impacts of its activities, products or services.* " Likewise, planning has to reflect the realities of an organization's environmental position. All significant environmental aspects must be factored into the organization's plan.

Although Section 4.2a mentions activities, products, and services, this does not necessarily mean that evaluations have to be exhaustive, covering every possible aspect of every product. For many companies, such an activity could become so detailed that it could preclude the possibility of ever arriving at a workable EMS. Representative categories of products and services may be selected, and environmental impacts may be inferred from these more general categories. Also, in the example of new site construction, the activity may be a temporary one that can be managed short-term.

The international standard also recognizes that, in the case of a supplier who contributes parts to a larger consumer end-item, the organization's control over design, disposal of the product, and other environmental aspects may be quite limited. The standard only expects you to control what you can control. Legal obligations in some areas, however, may call for you to go far beyond what might seem reasonable to the average person on the street—ISO 14000 does not, and cannot, give you relief from these obligations.

The fifth "shall" of the Specification (and the last one of Section 4.3.1) requires that this information be kept *"up-to-date."* Implicit in this requirement is a need for periodic review of an organization's environmental aspects—including review whenever new products, services, or activities are being added or deleted. The review must cover at least four key areas: legislative and regulatory requirements; identification of significant environmental aspects; examination of all existing environmental-management practices and procedures; and an evaluation of data gleaned from the investigation of previous incidents. A "what if" attitude should be adopted, so normal, abnormal, and emergency situations are all factored into the organization's planning.

4.3.2 *Legal and other requirements (4.2.2)*

In the sixth mandatory element of the Specification, the organization is required to *"establish and maintain a procedure to identify and have access to legal and other requirements to which the organization subscribes . . . "* and further specifies that this includes all requirements *" . . . that are applicable to the environmental aspects of its activities, products or services."*

Basically, this section reinforces the traditional position that "ignorance of the law is no excuse," and it makes each organization responsible for staying aware of the environmental laws, regulations, and controls that affect it.

And it goes beyond that. The language, *" . . . and other requirements to which the organization subscribes . . . "* means that industry-association environmental standards, corporate environmental dictates, environmental issues in union agreements, agreements with public authorities, nonregulatory guidelines, and similar voluntary ascriptions have virtually the same weight as law in the eyes of Section 4.3.2. All must be identified and tracked.

There are two methods of doing this. If your organization has the resources, a database may be designed to identify, track, and update requirements. Or you can subscribe to a service that will do the job for you. Either method will fulfill the requirements of the Specification. If your organization is entrepreneurial, you may choose to develop a database and then share your findings with others in your industry for a fee. Or, as an EMS objective, you can share that database with others non-gratis.

Either way, once the requirements are identified, construction of a simple matrix, listing requirements on the left side of a sheet, with the method intended to satisfy that requirement listed on the right will help you audit your legal requirements. Such a matrix identifies unfulfilled requirements, at a glance, so lapses can be swiftly rectified.

4.3.3 *Objectives and targets (4.2.3)*

Three more mandatory elements emerge here. This section compels your organization to " . . . *establish and maintain documented environmental objectives and targets . . .* " and goes on to require that type of diligence " . . . *at each relevant function and level within the organization.*"

The Specification lists factors that must be considered as this is done: " . . . *legal and other requirements, . . . significant environmental aspects, . . . technological options and . . . financial, operational and business requirements and the views of interested parties.*" Finally, Section 4.3.3 requires that objectives and targets be " . . . *consistent with the environmental policy, including the commitment to prevention of pollution.*"

If you refer back to the definitions of "objectives" and "targets," you'll see that such things should be measurable; this implies that documentation of such measurement will be required to prove progress and continual improvement.

Preventive measures should be taken into account, wherever possible. The use of best management practices (BMP) and best available technologies (BAT) is highly encouraged—so long as the organization can justify it from a financial standpoint.

Along these lines, the phrase " . . . *financial, operational and business requirements . . .* " reflects the real-world views of the businesspeople who authored ISO 14000 and should by no means be taken as an "out" for glossing over any bona fide objective or target. Don't take this as an implication that environmental cost-accounting methods are a requirement—they are not. The Specification recognizes that businesses must be sustainable, so a livable standard was written to encourage subscribers to stay the course, and not abandon their environmental efforts in the face of financial pressures.

4.3.4 *Environmental management programs (4.2.4)*

Four mandatory elements are embodied in this section. One is the obvious requirement to " . . . *establish and maintain (a) program(s) for achieving . . . objectives and targets.* " Note the word "maintain"—documentation will be required here.

Another mandatory element (4.3a) specifies that programs designate specific individuals or job titles responsible for achieving each objective and target, as well as (4.3b) the way in which they are to be achieved and deadlines for doing so.

Section 4.3.4 recognizes that business, technologies, and business offerings all change as part of the natural life cycle of an organization, so the last mandatory element in this section specifies that programs should be amended to accommodate such developments or deletions in activities, products, and services.

Standard operating procedure is to use a matrix to set up plans: Regulations and requirements go in the lead column, followed by objectives, targets, persons responsible, means of accomplishment, and the date or time frame for accomplishing each step. For long-term projects, a sheet should be drawn up for each requirement, with a roster of gradual steps illustrated, demonstrating how the organization will show progress of the program or continual improvement in each area.

It is customary in program design to consider all stages in the life of a product, service, or activity: planning, design, production, marketing, and disposal. Adapt this list where necessary—for products, consider materials; for facilities planning, consider construction techniques.

You'll note that, as I've gone over this part of the Specification, I've often said "programs," as opposed to "program." You *should* have a program for each functional area of your company. If you choose to have just one, it is permissible to subdivide it/them into several elements as necessary for evaluation and communication. The object is to craft an EMS that fits into the way that you do business, not to try forcing your company to follow an ill-fitting plan. Write something that you can work with.

4.4 *Implementation and operation (4.3)*

The implementation and operation portion of the Specification is the mother lode of mandatory elements. Nineteen separate requirements—more than in any other area of the Specification—are listed here.

4.4.1 *Structure and responsibility (4.3.1)*

This part of the Specification calls on the organization to define the positions responsible for each program and program element. A matrix illustrating job titles and responsibilities, together with an EMS organizational chart, can provide the required documentation and communication of these responsibilities. This matrix can also be used for identifying training needs.

Management is required in this section to give the delegated positions the resources they need to do their jobs; these include " . . . *human resources and specialized skills, technology . . .* " and, of course, sufficient budget to get the job done.

Top management is particularly required here to appoint managers who will have clearly defined authorities for (4.4.1a) ensuring conformance to the ISO 14000 international standard and (4.4.1b) *"reporting on the performance of the environmental management system to top management for review and as a basis for improvement of the environmental management system."*

The accepted interpretation of Section 4.4.1 is that each organization appoint an environmental management system coordinator who is responsible for facilitating the implementation of the EMS and for reporting progress to top management. In turn, various people (who generally have other job responsibilities as well) will develop and oversee different elements of the system and report and document their activities to the coordinator. The coordinator becomes the point person for interaction with the audit team leader when environmental-management-system audits are performed. Many companies refer to this coordinator as the management representative.

Ultimately, environmental responsibility falls on every person in the organization. Environmental accountability becomes part of each job title in an ISO 14000 company— it is there in the background in every decision made, every job that is done.

Environmental responsibility is like fire and safety responsibility: You may have a safety committee and possibly even a fire-fighting staff on board at your facility, but that in no way lessens anyone's obligation to work in a safe manner and guard against fires. When your trash can starts smoking, the prudent thing to do is to find a fire extinguisher before the thing erupts into flames—not merely send an e-mail to the fire-safety supervisor. In the same manner, everyone, in every position, every day has to step up to his or her own personal responsibility for preventing and correcting environmental impacts. ISO 14000 makes environmental management part of the company operations, and the right attitude ensures success.

4.4.2 *Training, awareness and competence (4.3.2)*

The training requirements for ISO 9000 and ISO 14000 are quite similar. Both standards mandate the organization to identify training needs and to assure appropriate training. In the case of ISO 14000, that training is required for " . . . *all personnel whose work may create a significant impact upon the environment. . . .* "

People such as oil-tanker captains, hazardous-material truck drivers, and nuclear reactor control-room operators all perform jobs that may create a significant environmental impact. But so do the people who fuel your company's fleet (and can cause spills or create emissions to the air or water in the process), the people who operate cranes or lift trucks (and can drop or knock over environmentally sensitive materials) or even the people who care for your lawns (and may introduce undesirable levels of fertilizers or pesticides into the local aquifer). And *everyone* must understand the environment policy and ISO 14001 intent. So a "long view" of potential impacts is necessary.

In the cradle-to-grave perspective required by ISO 14000, your organization will also require its *contractors* to verify that their employees have had the environmental training needed for safe operations, as demanded by your

EMS. Everyone working on your organization's behalf has to be pulling in the same direction.

Employees need to know the importance of conforming with the environmental policy and its procedures (4.4.2a); the actual and potential environmental impacts of their work, together with the advantages of following the company's EMS procedures (4.4.2b); what, specifically, they should be doing to help achieve the organization's environmental goals—including what they should be doing in the event of any particular environmental emergency (4.4.2c); and the consequences of not following standard operating procedures (4.4.2d).

Training is a subject that deserves close attention and diligence. Since it is the segment of your EMS that will require the most fallow employee hours and that will affect the largest segment of your workforce, training is also generally the most costly element of an EMS (with nonsalaried workers, you pay not only for training, but also for the hours your people spend off the job and in training). With care, training will yield dividends in reduced waste and lower cost of impacts, but proper budget planning is necessary to keep training liabilities from overwhelming the rest of the organization's environmental resources.

ISO 14001 Section 4.4.2 closes with the requirement that individuals holding jobs with a potential for environmental impact " . . . *shall be competent on the basis of appropriate education, training and/or experience.*" This requirement creates a need for a three- or four-element matrix for each position, indicating the job title (i.e., "crane operator"), education or experience requirements ("high school or GED diploma and three years experience as an apprentice operator"), required training ("SPC, simple EMS awareness, basic safety procedures, problem solving, and hazardous material handling"), timetable for such training ("first week of each quarter"), and targeted completion date for training ("within 90 days for both new hires and promotions"). Such matrices become part of an organization's overall EMS documentation.

Who determines how much training and how much education is enough? External forces (unions, apprenticeship programs, etc.) may influence this, but generally such matters are management's decision. However, management (through the review process) is responsible for verifying the effectiveness and adequacy of training programs and demonstrating both in the audit process.

4.4.3 *Communication (4.3.3)*

Compartmentalization has no place in an ISO 14000 environmental management system. The Specification calls for organizations to establish and maintain procedures for (4.4.3a) *"internal communication . . . "* and (4.4.3b) *"receiving, documenting and responding to relevant communication from external interested parties."*

The communication from external parties is apt to take the form of letters of complaint. There was a story about the fellow who, while traveling across the continent by train, pulled back the sheets on his Pullman bed to find a cockroach scurrying away. Outraged, he wrote a letter to the president of the railroad, and promptly the following week, he received a letter that read, "Dear Sir: We are perplexed and dismayed at the recent problem you encountered, concerning cockroaches in one of our fine railway carriages. We understand your concern and can only tell you that we are as surprised as you by this lapse in standards. Please rest assured that we have pulled that car from the line and dismantled it. It will be completely fumigated and checked before being reassembled and placed back into service."

The letter was signed by the president of the railroad, and the disgruntled customer was feeling quite placated until a slip of paper dropped out of the railway company's envelope. On it were scribbled the words, "Jack—send this @#$!&% the cockroach letter."

Lest there be any confusion on the matter, consider the following to be an inflexible rule: Your external communications regarding your organization's environmental position cannot be limited to "the cockroach letter."

Response to external communications must be relevant, and the situation triggering the external communication must be documented and kept on file as an environmental impact. The situation generating the communication should be weighed when determining your organization's objective and targets. EMS audit teams are trained to look for links between external communications and management review, and to regard with suspicion any system that is particularly lacking in such links.

Sometimes, situations may merit more than a letter of reply. If you have a community group voicing a concern, or a party raising a complex issue, you may elect to hold a dialogue—or even an ongoing discussion—to address those concerns. Sometimes documentation—assessments of particular environmental aspects or impacts or details of emergency planning—are the best way to answer concerns. The standard expects your organization to not only acknowledge and respond to enquiries, but to take an interest in the environmental issues the enquiries concern.

In addition, the specification requires an organization to " . . . *consider processes for external communication on its significant environmental aspects and record that position.*"

This mandatory element encourages *proactive,* as well as reactive, external communications. Reports, public document records, product information sheets, paid advertising, partnerships with non-profit organizations, news releases, and public appearances by top management can all serve as external communication. External communication, if properly managed and executed, can be a positive, rewarding and (better still) margin-generating experience, as will be discussed in Chapter 11.

4.4.4 *Environmental management system documentation (4.3.4)*

The 24th mandatory element of ISO 14001 is—not surprisingly, given the priority accorded documentation throughout the Specification—a requirement for the organization to " . . . *establish and maintain information . . .* " that describes (4.4.4a) " *. . . the core elements of the environmental management system and their interaction"* and provides (4.4.4b) *" . . . direction to related documentation."*

This documentation, which provides a road map to an organization's EMS, may be maintained in either electronic or paper form. Most companies will elect to do both since, once an organization has established the former (i.e., word-processed it into the computer), it is usually a simple matter to generate the latter. Contrary to popular belief, this documentation does not have to take the form of a single environmental manual—some multiprogram systems or multilevel organizations may find that too awkward an approach. Some small organizations may believe a manual to be unnecessary paperwork.

Examples of *"related documentation"* include such things as report forms, process information, organizational charts, internal standards and standard operating procedures, and site-specific emergency plans.

4.4.5 *Document control (4.3.5)*

If your company has a document-control protocol to satisfy the requirements of ISO 9001, you already have a system in place that will satisfy the document-control needs of the environmental Specification, as well. This is just one of the reasons it is so cost-effective to implement ISO 14000 into a company that is already ISO 9000-certified.

Procedures for controlling documents under the ISO 14001 Specification include five requirements (all grouped under the 25th "shall" of Clause 4). These include requirements that documents: (4.4.5a) " . . . *can be located";* (4.4.5b) " . . . *are periodically reviewed, revised as necessary and approved . . . by authorized personnel";* that copies of current documents (4.4.5c) " . . . *are available at all locations . . . "* where they might be needed; (4.4.5d) that *"obsolete documents are promptly removed from all points of issue and points of use . . . "* or that steps are taken to prevent their unintended use; and (4.4.5e) *"any obsolete documents retained for legal and/or knowledge preservation purposes are suitably identified"* (i.e., stamped with a warning label or otherwise prominently marked in a manner which will prevent even those unfamiliar with the documents from using them by mistake).

Two additional mandatory elements close out this section of the Specification. ISO 14001 also calls for documents to be legible (which may require typewriter or computer transcription of handwritten records), dated at creation and each revision, identifiable, and " . . . *maintained in an orderly manner and retained for a specified period . . . "* (how long you retain documents depends on the nature of your business or on established regulatory requirements). For example, records of superfund sites must be retained 25 years, while waste manifests should be kept indefinitely. However, audit reports need only be kept through one audit cycle. The Specification also requires each organization to establish standard procedures for the creation and modification of documents.

One concern is that in ISO 14000, as in ISO 9000, it is possible to get so wrapped up in documentation that the system winds up nothing more than a slave to paper serving its own fulfillment more than its environmental goals. As the saying goes, "When you are up to your waist in alligators, you may forget that the mission is to drain the swamp."

Remember that records are there to serve your EMS needs—not the other way around. Keep your process short and simple. When records begin to overwhelm you, it is time to exercise one of the principles of continual improvement and simplify and streamline your records process. Document adequately, but do not allow yourself to become enmeshed in documentation. Auditors will look for specific types of records when examining your EMS system, and these will be discussed later in the book.

4.4.6 *Operational control (4.3.6)*

Two mandatory elements of Section 4.4.6 are the requirements to " . . . *identify those operations and activities that are associated with the identified significant environmental aspects . . .* " and to " . . . *plan these activities, including maintenance, in order to ensure that they are carried out under specified conditions. . . .* " Those conditions include:

4.4.6a "establishing and maintaining documented procedures . . . " *to cover situations that could threaten the integrity of the organization's environmental policy, objectives and targets*

4.4.6b "stipulating operating criteria . . . " *in each documented procedure, and*

4.4.6c *establishing procedures relevant to the* " . . . identifiable significant environmental aspects of goods and services used by the organization . . . " *and* *making sure that these procedures are known and understood by the vendors and contractors responsible for them.*

The only way to thoroughly identify every applicable element of your organization's daily operations is to do a process flow analysis (i.e., identify process activities and critical environmental junctures). This is similar to the process used in identifying quality issues of operational control for ISO 9000.

4.4.7 *Emergency preparedness and response (4.3.7)*

As has been noted, there are parallels between ISO 9000 and ISO 14000; the ISO 14001 Specification is patterned after ISO 9001.

Section 4.4.7 is an exception to this analogous nature of the two Specifications. Because breakdowns in quality management rarely create an immediate threat to life, property, or resources in or around the organization, emergency-preparedness-and-response provisions are unnecessary in ISO 9001.

A quick review of environmental news coverage demonstrates the need for emergency provisions in any environmental management system. Not only does the capability to handle emergencies help prevent harm to the environment, it also helps protect your organization's environmental reputation because negative news is far more likely to get coverage than positive emergency preparedness and response.

There are three mandatory elements to this section (30, 31, and 32). They include requirements to " . . . *establish and maintain procedures to identify potential for and respond to accidents and emergency situations . . . "*; to " . . . *review and revise . . . "* procedures where necessary after an accident or emergency has occurred (a real-world test of the procedure); and to *" . . . periodically test such procedures where practicable."*

Procedural tests are generally drills involving staged or mock emergencies. As a rule of thumb, you should plan on performing such drills annually—or more often if it appears necessary to do so to maintain an adequate state of preparation. Where practical should be interpreted strictly. While you should not stage a fire for practice, you should expect to stop production as necessary to perform such a drill. Failure to do so would result in a nonconformance.

4.5 *Checking and corrective action (4.4)*

Everything covered thus far about the ISO 14001 Specification has been *strategic:* It has involved planning and setting elements in place for future activity.

Section 4.5 is a departure from this pattern. It introduces the *tactical* aspects of ISO 14001, those facets of the Specification that address actual, real-world application of the plan and the means of addressing deviations from stated practices or ensuring changes needed to achieve specific results. Deviations are referred to as nonconformances in the standard.

4.5.1 *Monitoring and measurement (4.4.1)*

As mentioned earlier, environmental objectives and targets should be quantifiable whenever possible, and environmental performance should be gauged by *"measurable results."* This section of the Specification lists four mandatory elements pertaining to monitoring and measurement.

One is the requirement to *" . . . establish and maintain documented procedures to monitor and measure . . . key characteristics of . . . operations and activities that can have a significant impact on the environment."* This activity must be regular, and measurements must be recorded *" . . . to track performance, relevant operational controls and conformance."* Normally, an EMS will call for specific people (by job titles) to perform measurements at regular intervals (monthly, weekly, daily, hourly, etc.). Measurements include outputs (emissions and discharges), progress (meeting of program goals) and overall management and performance.

The Specification also calls for the maintenance and calibration of equipment used to monitor outputs—and records must be kept of these services.

The fourth, and final monitoring-and-measurement requirement calls for the establishment and maintenance of " . . . *a documented procedure for periodically evaluating compliance with relevant environmental legislation and regulations.*" Again, the EMS should specify who is responsible in each area for assuring that all legal and regulatory requirements have been identified, monitored and measured levels are in accordance with all pertinent regulations, and that all reports filed with regulatory bodies were complete and timely.

4.5.2 *Nonconformance and corrective and preventive action (4.4.2)*

In the 37th mandatory element of the Specification, organizations are directed to assign responsibility for ensuring conformance, and to grant authority to responsible parties to investigate nonconformances (situations which do not correspond to the standard). Authorized parties are to take action to " . . . *mitigate any impacts caused . . .* " and to take corrective action.

The scale of this corrective action needs to be (38th mandatory element) in keeping with the magnitude of the actual or potential nonconformance—you don't go after a major oil spill with a roll of paper towels; and (mandatory element 39) the organization is required to " . . . implement and record any changes in the documented procedures . . . " that result from the corrective or preventive action. Changes need not be documented until corrective action has been proven effective.

The way to successfully satisfy this section of the Specification is to "identify, implement and record." For any given situation, you (1) identify the cause of the nonconformance; (2) identify and implement the corrective measure; (3) implement those controls necessary to avoid repetition of the nonconformance and verify their effectiveness; and (4) record any written procedure changes necessitated by the corrective action.

Don't overdocument (see comments in Section 4.4.5), but do document the nonconformance sufficiently to answer future questions.

4.5.3 *Records (4.4.3)*

Since objective documentation is a requirement of both ISO 9000 and ISO 14000, it should surprise no one that the records requirements for Checking and Corrective Action are fairly exacting. Only three paragraphs long in the International Specification, Section 4.5.3 contains six mandatory elements.

In language that brings to mind that of Section 4.4.5 (Document Control), the Specification calls for organizations to "... *establish and maintain procedures for the identification, maintenance and disposal of environmental records.*" It then lists examples of such records, including "... *training records and the results of audits and reviews.*"

The Specification calls for records to be legible, identifiable, and traceable to the originating activity, product, or service. They should be readily retrievable, but stored in a manner that protects "... *against damage, deterioration or loss.*" The latter can be accomplished by keeping duplicate sets of records in two different locations, backing up records on computers, and using other data-protection technologies.

Here is a listing of potential environmental records considered by the authors of ISO 14001:

➤ Information on applicable environmental laws and regulations.

➤ Complaint records.

➤ Training records including the verification of the effectiveness of training.

➤ Process information including impact identification.

➤ Product information.

➤ Inspection, maintenance, and calibration records.

➤ Pertinent contractor and supplier information.

➤ Incident reports and corrective actions written in response.

➤ Information regarding emergency preparedness and response including records of drills.

➤ Records indicating how environmental aspects were identified and ranked.

➤ Audit results.

➤ Follow-up on corrective actions.

➤ Management review records including evaluation of technological options and consideration of environmental aspects when planning expansion.

The length of time records should be kept varies, and will be determined in large part by the retention time demanded in state and federal regulations, liability in employee safety, and audit and management review cycles.

4.5.4 *Environmental management system audit (4.4.4)*

At least annually, an organization needs to internally audit its EMS, to determine whether it conforms to both the organization's plan and the international standard, and whether the EMS has been implemented properly and is operating effectively. Results of this audit are to be provided to management for the purpose of review and possible changes.

The internal audit procedures for ISO 14000 are quite similar to those for ISO 9000, with one exception. While the implications of a quality initiative are generally obvious or intuitive, the same cannot always be said of the elements of an EMS, so environmental management system auditors will generally need to have specialized environmental training to complete their tasks.

According to the authors if ISO 14001, your audit program should spell out:

➤ Activities and areas to be considered.

➤ Audit frequency.

➤ Associated responsibilities.

➤ Communication of results.

➤ Auditor competence.

➤ How audits will be conducted.

The type of audit performed should be appropriate to the scale of the activity and the potential environmental impacts involved, given the organizations's activities, products, or services. Auditors, whether internal or external, should be in a position to do their jobs impartially and objectively; for example, they should not be members of the party that set up or implemented the environmental management system being audited. Use common sense.

The issue of auditor competence is tricky. Quality auditors may or may not be good candidates for training as EMS auditors. They will certainly require additional training in environmental aspects and impacts.

4.6 *Management review (4.5)*

The management review clause addresses the responsibilities of top management ("top" is *top,* the organization's most senior managers), and spells out four mandatory elements for management review: At intervals that it determines, management must review the EMS to ensure it remains adequate for the situation at hand, is effective, and in conformance to ISO 14001 standard. To make this possible, sufficient information must be gathered and placed at management's disposal, and the review must be documented (this document will be requested by most external audit teams).

Although management reviews should be comprehensive, it is not necessary to review all elements of the EMS at once. The review process may also be spread out over a manageable time period.

According to ISO 14001, reviews should include:

1. Audit results including the status and effectiveness of corrective actions.

2. Measurements of success in reaching objectives or targets.

3. Gauges of the continuing suitability of the EMS as it stands.

4. The concerns of relevant interested parties.

The purpose of a management review is to determine whether the EMS needs to be changed, revised, or updated to continue to do its job.

Just as various elements within an environmental management system gradually improve ("raising the bar" as time goes on), so the EMS should improve over time as well. Management review closes one complete cycle of policy, planning, implementation, checking, and review, and opens another. A good EMS is in a continual state of evolution, constantly becoming a *better* EMS.

Implementing Your Environmental Management System

There's always an easy solution to every problem—
neat, plausible, and wrong.

—H.L. Mencken

Why do you need a systemic approach to environmental management?

Because, whether you think about it or not, you are already operating within an ecosystem, an environment in which every action, every expenditure of energy, every process, product, and by-product, is integral to, and affects, the whole.

To explain this total interrelationship, quantum physicists use a concept called "chaos theory." It's called the chaos theory, not because everything is in chaos, but because in an ecosystem as large as Earth, every act affects the whole. A butterfly flapping its wings in Tokyo affects the winds that blow over Gary, Indiana. A tree falling in a Brazilian rain forest is recorded in a change of air's oxygen content readings in Boston. It's called chaos theory because any such intricately interrelated ecosystem includes countless billions of factors, too many variables to put into any viable equation. So to us, it appears chaotic. It is not.

Chaos theory suggests two realities. First, only a holistic approach to the environment makes sense. Yet individual governments pass laws and regulations that address only a single, isolated aspect of the whole. We act as if world population growth, deforestation, soil erosion, acid precipitation, ozone layer depletion, global climatic change, material recycling, resource conservation, and habitat protection are separate issues. We act as though environmental concerns can be separated from all the other realities of life, making no effort to integrate tax policies, urban planning, and government incentives into a total equation. Governments regulate industry without consideration of how the legislation will affect markets and jobs, thus inviting the dual evils of poverty and hunger, which fuel and frustrate all other environmental efforts. Our global behavior makes no sense.

Only a holistic approach to an environment makes sense. And that's as true when you're talking about your small company's environment, or when you are talking about the Earth. The first and foremost task of senior management is to attempt to see your company's environmental system in the larger context of your community, your country, and your world. This may seem like an impossible task, and yet your overall environmental policies will only stand the test of time if they make sense in a far larger context.

Second, managing your company's environment also requires a holistic approach. An environmental management system takes into account everyone's responsibilities, practices, procedures, processes, the renewability of required resources, the long-term effects over time, recycling costs—everything for an organization to *implement* and *maintain* a manageable operation.

A systems approach allows an organization to control activities that may impact the environment and to determine to what extent it is satisfying regulatory and legislative requirements, as well as its own stated environmental objectives. The management structure can assist organizations in meeting their environmental objectives, and socioeconomic expectations. In a sense, it allows you to integrate your company and goals with those of the society as a whole.

Establishing an EMS is the foundation of implementing the ISO 14000 series. As such, the *ISO 14001: Environmental Management Systems and Specification* standard is considered to be the core document of the series. It will also be the foundation on which the organization's environmental management system is built.

There are five other documents in the environmental series for use in establishing and guiding the EMS:

1. *Environmental Auditing* provides a road map for the environmental auditing process.

2. *Environmental Performance Evaluation* is the tenet of organizational evaluation of environmental performance.

3. *Life-Cycle Assessment* gives the organization definitive guidance in cradle-to-grave evaluation in choosing product materials for organizational purchases and production.

4. *Environmental Labels and Declarations* outlines ISO 14000's guidelines for environmental marketing claims—truth in advertising.

5. And finally, *Environmental Aspects in Product Standards* provides assistance in rating of organizational products.

There's an old saying in business that "what gets measured, gets done." Documentation is the organization's validation of measurement, proving that your environmental management system is in place and operates as you claim. When completed, the EMS documentation will consist of:

➤ An environmental policy.

➤ An environmental manual (optional).

➤ Written procedures.

➤ Written work instructions (where required).

➤ Supporting records.

Supporting records will vary from organization to organization. The records are based in part on the governmental regulations that apply to environmental activities of the organization such as forms for emission and discharge monitoring. Other examples of supporting records include: evaluations of suppliers; communications from external interested parties; employee training information; environmental objectives and targets; and a written management program for implementing the objectives.

Figure 6-1 illustrates EMS documentation viewed as a three-tiered model.

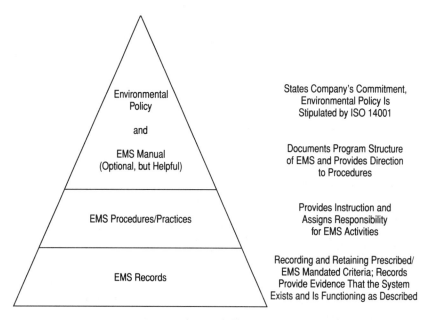

Figure 6-1. Environmental Management System Pyramid

■ ESTABLISHING AN ENVIRONMENTAL MANAGEMENT SYSTEM DEMANDS COMMITMENT

Establishing an Environmental Management System involves considerable effort, and its success depends on commitment from all levels of an organization, particularly top management. The majority of people in an organization will take their cue from their leaders. And since ISO 14001 is first and foremost a *management system,* the company leadership must define not only the expectations, but the attitude about environmental management.

ISO 14001 states the expectation of the standard: Top management must define the organization's intent to prevent/minimize environment pollution, willingly provide all necessary support actions, and demonstrate organizational commitment to continual improvement of the environmental management system. The organization will fail in its commitment to the ISO 14000 standards if management does not promote that commitment, or even appears only halfhearted in its support.

Management's first task is to appoint one or more management representatives. The higher the rank your environmental manager holds in your organization, the more support you are giving environmental concern. To gain maximum results, you should assign the position to someone high enough in your organization to provide your program with credibility and authority. As an example, many companies today combine environmental management, quality, health, and safety, to create a large enough bailiwick to justify a vice presidential appointment. This gives tremendous status to the effort and also underscores the interrelationship of these closely related areas of concern.

The management representative will have a defined role with responsibilities and authority for ensuring that the environmental management system is established, implemented, and maintained by the organization as required by the ISO 14001 standards. Other responsibilities of the management representative include acting as the liaison between operations and top management so that identified resource needs for the environmental management system are met and reporting to the organization's top management on the EMS operations so they can be reviewed and continually improved.

You're way ahead of the process if your organization currently has an environmental management system, as less effort will be required to become registered. The key to implementing ISO 14001 is that the organization's current management system and practices need not be discarded, but should be adapted into an ISO 14001 system.

■ BUILDING AN ENVIRONMENTAL MANAGEMENT SYSTEM

In creating an environmental management system, you must articulate an environmental policy that summarizes the organization's philosophy toward the environment. This policy must meet the requirements of ISO 14001 as outlined in Section 4.2.

Once the policy is established, the organization's environmental aspects (activities, products, and services that can interact with the environment), must be defined by the organization's management team.

To do this, a program for identifying environmental impacts needs to be developed. These environmental impacts include any change to the environment—positive or negative—and can be caused by all or part of the organization's activities, processes, products, or services. For example, building a new facility in a suburban area could severely strain the community wastewater treatment system's ability to meet the demands created by heavy industrial discharge during major rainstorms. This would create a negative impact. On the other hand, if the local municipality mandated the organization build a storm-water retention pond on site, the organization could landscape the area to support migrating wildlife.

A thorough, systematic review of the organization's current management system controlling environmental practices should be undertaken. This system's practices must be compared with the principles outlined in ISO 14001, and any differences between the current practices and the requirements of ISO 14001 can then be identified and addressed.

How much environmental structure you already have will depend on how much or little you've been "blessed" with government regulation up until now. Some organizations will have no current environmental practices, as they have no processes or activities that are regulated by a government agency. Other organizations, such as medical equipment manufacturers, are heavily regulated, so they will have much of the structure needed to create an environmental management system already in place.

An optional EMS manual can be written incorporating the organization's general mission and environmental vision. It will include its environmental policy and present the organization's intent to implement and maintain the six elements of the ISO 14001 standard. The manual provides direction to the documentation needed for operation and support of the environmental management system. This need not be a long document. Remember these are the policies—the operating philosophies—that you want everyone in your organization to buy into and support. The clearer, the more concise, the better. It is useful to remember that the U.S. Declaration of Independence contains only 1,322 words. So why does anyone need a hundred thousand words to define a company's environmental vision?

More detail needs to come with the procedures that are written to define practices. Some procedures can be developed in an all-inclusive style, meaning they provide all of the "how-to" directions needed to complete that procedure. Other procedures will be an overall view of related environmental activities within a department and will require separate work instructions. These, in turn, will outline how to conduct each specific activity called for by the procedure.

The organization will rank the impacts of their activities on the environment, and then will prioritize them according to selected criteria to select environmental objectives and targets. An environmental management program should be created to define, execute, and measure the objectives and targets chosen.

Essential to the system is that you build review into the basic procedures. You need to develop review of all the EMS documentation at designated intervals, and adopt a process for making necessary operational changes in documented procedures.

Here are the principles, summarized from the elements of ISO 14001, that must be incorporated into the environmental management system:

1. An environmental policy must be established and maintained. This policy must meet the six "shalls" stated in Section 4.2 of the ISO 14001 specification standard. Highlights of this subsection include a commitment to:

   ➤ Meet applicable legislative and regulatory requirements.

   ➤ Achieve continual improvement (by identifying opportunities for improvement).

   ➤ Minimize or prevent pollution.

1A. An optional EMS manual may be established and maintained, describing the environmental management system (4.4.4). This manual:

➤ May address the organization's mission and environmental vision statements.

➤ Will address its environmental policy statements and present the organization's intent to meet the six (6) elements of the ISO 14001 specification standard.

➤ Will also provide direction to the documentation needed to implement and support the environmental management system.

2. Procedures must be established and maintained to identify:

➤ Environmental aspects of those activities, products, and services that could potentially interact with the environment (4.3.1).

➤ Environmental legal and regulatory requirements (4.3.2).

3. Environmental objectives and targets must be documented (4.3.3).

4. An environmental management program must be established and maintained to assist the organization in achieving its environmental objectives and targets (4.3.4).

5. Roles, responsibilities, and authorities for the implementation and maintenance of the environmental management system must be defined, documented, and communicated (4.4.1).

6. All resources necessary to design, implement, and maintain the environmental management system (both monetary and human) must be identified and provided (4.4.1).

7. A management representative (MR) must be appointed to oversee the environmental management system and all related activities (4.4.1).

8. Training needs for the successful operation of the environmental management system must be identified and provided to employees. Training procedures are required (4.4.2).

9. Procedures must be established and maintained to support internal and external environmental communications (4.4.3).

10. Procedures must be created, maintained, and controlled for EMS documents. This includes such matters as operating procedures, environmental records, training records, and results of audits and reviews. (4.4.5).

11. Procedures must be established and maintained to control those operations and activities that could create significant environmental impacts (4.4.6).

12. Procedures must be in place providing direction on how the organization is to respond to emergency situations. These procedures should address ways to prevent or minimize environmental impacts that could result from accidents or emergency situations (4.4.7).

13. Procedures must be in place to monitor and measure operations and activities that may have significant environmental impacts (4.5.1).

14. Procedures must be established and maintained for investigating and initiating corrective and preventive actions (4.5.2).

15. Procedures must be established and maintained for the identification, maintenance, and disposition of environmental records (4.5.3).

16. Periodic audits must be carried out on the environmental management system to determine:

    ➤ Whether the system has been properly implemented.

    ➤ Whether desired requirements are being met. Documented auditing procedures are required (4.5.4).

17. Top management must conduct regular reviews of the environmental management system to ensure its continued suitability and effectiveness (4.6).

These add up to a lot of "musts" for a voluntary system, but they are all essential to control the process and eliminate oversights. The beauty of a system is integration of elements, and when this one is put together properly, your environmental management system should help to prevent, or at least minimize, negative environmental impacts and their associated costs.

■ THE ENVIRONMENTAL POLICY

The environmental policy provides a clear, accurate picture of the organization's beliefs and activities of environmental management. Usually no more than one or two pages in length, the policy should be clear and concise. Customers, investors, employees, or other interested parties reading the document should easily discern the following:

➤ The organization's environmental vision and guiding principles having approval and support by top-level management.

➤ The environmental policy's relevance to the organization's operations, products, and services.

➤ The organization's key commitments (e.g., prevention of pollution, fulfilling legal requirements).

➤ The organization's intent to communicate the policy to all internal and external parties.

➤ The organization's commitment to continual improvement.

The organization should always remember that the policy has two main objectives: organizational direction and communication of organizational intent to external interested parties. The policy is a marketing tool and should be designed to make a good first impression. Sincerity and specifity are vital.

The environmental policy can also indicate organizational goals such as an intent to keep abreast of relevant technology and management practices for enhancing performance evaluation procedures and related indicators.

➤ Incorporation of Life-Cycle Thinking

Cradle-to-grave environmental management calls for consideration at every stage of a product's life, and in all stages of your organization's activities. Some points worth remembering are:

➤ Minimizing the significant harmful environmental impacts of new development by using integrated environmental management planning and policies.

➤ Designing products to keep their environmental impacts in production, use, and disposal to a minimum.

➤ Preventing and avoiding pollution, decreasing waste and the use of resources (i.e., materials, fuel, and energy), and pledging to recover and recycle when possible.

➤ Supporting training and education.

➤ Relaying environmental experience to others.

➤ Involving interested parties.

➤ Striving to operate with fewer raw materials.

➤ Urging suppliers and contractors to establish an EMS.

If you regularly have contractors working on site, they must receive training as well, for your environmental management system to be in compliance with ISO 14000.

➤ The Environmental Management System Manual

ISO 14001 stipulates the description of the environmental management system under Section 4.4.4, but the amount of information given by the organization in that description is at the discretion of the organization. The breadth and width of the description must meet the organization's need. A formal EMS manual is optional. A company as large and as diversified as Ford Motor Company, in the process of registering 126 facilities, will require a more extensively documented system than will Great Lakes Box Corporation, which currently has one facility, no regulated processes, and less than one hundred employees. Each company must make a choice based on its needs.

The EMS manual can provide a focus that the organization's system might not otherwise have. If included, it can serve the environmental management system in much the same way that a quality manual serves a quality system.

If an organization chooses to prepare an EMS manual, it should address the organization's commitment to meet all six (6) elements of ISO 14001, as well as list the responsibilities, procedures, and records associated with each element.

The organization's commitment to the ISO 14001 elements can easily be addressed by turning the mandatory "shalls" of the standard into "we do" statements. For example, as a part of the EMS manual, Section 4.4.4—Environmental Management System Documentation—would change from:

> The organization shall establish and maintain information, in paper or electronic form: a) describe the core elements of the management system and their interaction; and b) provide direction to related documentation.

to:

> The ABC Corporation has established and maintains information to describe the core elements of its management system and the interaction of and between those elements. Directions to related documents are referenced in our Environmental Management System Manual.

The EMS manual can serve numerous other functions. It:

➤ Aids in the creation and implementation of an environmental management system.

➤ Describes the structure of the environmental management system.

➤ Explains the framework and goals of the environmental management system.

➤ Demonstrates management's commitment to the system.

➤ Serves as a cross-reference to the environmental management system and the ISO 14000 standard.

➤ Serves as a cross-reference to the facility procedures.

➤ Serves as an EMS reference document for auditors and other designated parties (e.g., registrar, investors, customers).

Besides covering the appropriate sections of the ISO 14001 specification standard, the EMS manual can, and usually does, contain:

➤ A brief statement of the organization's commitment to continual improvement and the prevention/ minimization of pollution.

➤ A brief policy statement addressing the organization's environmental performance and reputation.

➤ A short organization profile that provides helpful background to interested external parties.

➤ A statement on how the organization plans to pursue its environmental objectives and targets.

➤ A list of all management positions or departmental locations possessing a copy of the environmental management manual.

➤ A list of facility procedures related to the six ISO 14001 elements.

➤ A statement of authority and responsibility.

The EMS manual should never be unwieldy or difficult to understand. If the readership could include employees at any level of the organization and interested external parties, care should be exercised to keep the document in an easy-to-read style using simple language. This is best accomplished by avoiding technical language, if possible, and complex numbering systems that may not be understood by someone unfamiliar with the ISO 14000 standards. An EMS manual need not be longer than about 25 pages.

Another alternative is to fuse your environmental stewardship and quality system into a single manual. This demonstrates the interrelationship of these systems, and it also saves paper. This will eliminate the need for an environmental management system manual. Remember that there are six elements in ISO 14001, and 20 elements in ISO 9001. The management system manual for organizations that merge the two systems must cover all 26 elements; it must present both quality and environmental policy in a manner that addresses both ISO 9000 Section 4.2.1 and ISO 14000 Section 4.2; and it must define responsibilities for both quality and environmental issues. Top management must commit to ensuring that both management systems are fully implemented and maintained.

■ IDENTIFYING ENVIRONMENTAL IMPACTS

We all have an effect on the environment. Driving a car, using the backyard grill, or mowing the lawn consumes human and motor energy, produce waste, and spew out minute chemical particles that interact with air, water, soil, and plants. While few dispute the right of people to engage in these enterprises, the question arises: "How do we learn to manage such activities and to minimize their impact on the environment?"

That's the same question you must ask about the activities of an organization—the processes it engages in, and the products and services it renders. Each operation has an impact on the environment to varying degrees. The potential for that impact must be identified and procedures written to demonstrate the organization's effort to control every environmental outcome.

Since you can never identify and write a procedure on everything, you will have to use discretion in defining the organization's normal and abnormal operations to determine which have significant potential impact.

Environmental aspects are defined as those elements within an organization's activities, products, and services that can significantly interact with the environment. Examples of environmental aspects would include manufacturing processes, raw material usage, waste products, and energy consumption. You should give consideration not only to actual interactions, but to all potential actions *especially potential emergency conditions.* Equally obvious, there is no point in identifying activities that management can have no control over. The real question in defining emergency conditions is: Can that action impact the environment, and can you control the impact? If you can't, then don't try to manage it.

A thorough review of the organization's departments, and the activities each engages in, can help identify those areas in which activities have potential for environmental impact. The findings will then be used to develop effective and suitable procedures to prevent or minimize pollution and to develop environmental awareness in employees and the community. Your organization's operations will dictate what activities can, or must, be covered by a procedure.

If the organization has an environmental management system in place already but is interested in upgrading the system to meet the ISO 14001 standard criteria, the review would take a slightly different approach. The existing system would be methodically audited to see whether it meets each mandatory "shall" in the ISO 14001 standard. The review would note gaps between the existing system and one meeting the ISO 14001 criteria. This is a "gap analysis" or baseline audit.

The gap analysis is a methodical exercise, and for it to be effective and complete, objective observers should conduct it. An organization can perform its own gap analysis using department or interdepartment personnel, or it can bring in a consultant who specializes in performing this review process. My experience is that an outside analyst at this juncture can more than earn his or her fees by seeing what insiders would simply not notice. It is very easy for organizations to overlook activities with a potential for environmental impact if the activity is unregulated or has never been perceived as a problem. Consultants who frequently audit systems to the ISO 14001 criteria are thoroughly versed in the standard and can more quickly and easily identify areas of an existing system that do not conform to the criteria.

Certain activities are obviously covered by the organization's environmental management system—those regulated by federal, state, or municipal environmental laws. These activities have significant environmental impact (or a high potential to have an impact) and therefore warrant legislation. Other key areas include:

➤ Addressing activities identified in union contracts.

➤ Addressing community concerns, such as migrating fowl or preservation of local watersheds.

➤ Choosing cleaning products for organizational housekeeping based on life-cycle considerations.

➤ Preventing and avoiding pollution by changes in management practices for groundskeeping (e.g., decrease the number of fertilizer applications on site).

➤ Limiting the significant harmful environmental impacts of new development by using integrated environmental management planning and policies.

➤ Embracing product design practices that incorporate cradle-to-grave concepts and minimize environmental impacts in production, use, and disposal.

➤ Decreasing use and waste of resources (e.g., paper products, electricity, water), and pledging to recover and recycle instead of dispose in administrative and employee lounge areas.

➤ Embracing environmental awareness philosophies in corporate philanthropical programs by supporting local educator training in balanced environmental education curricula for school teachers, scout and 4-H leaders, nature center, and day-care staff.

➤ Relaying environmental experience to others through professional affiliations and community activities.

➤ Urging suppliers and contractors to establish an environmental management system.

■ PROCEDURES

For each activity that is identified as having present or potential environmental impact, the organization must prepare written procedures to guide employee activity. *All* procedures will be in keeping with the values stated in the organization's EMS policy, and will be used by the environmental management system to satisfy the criteria of the ISO 14001 standards.

The policy and the manual (optional) are considered organization-level documents, outlining beliefs and practices that provide a focus for all organizational activity.

Senior management should be critically involved in developing and defining these documents. They represent the necessary environmental vision for your organization. Without an inspired and clearly articulated leadership vision, environmental management will flounder and, in time, fail.

Procedures

Everything should be as simple as possible, but no simpler.

—ALBERT EINSTEIN

P rocedures are where the lofty visions of environmental stewardship are translated into day-to-day departmental operations. The creation of a procedure is the point where idealism becomes practical considerations. It is at the procedural level where an environmental management system eventually either works or fails.

While the environmental management system policy deals with concepts, the procedure is activity based. It describes how an activity (or set of actions) is performed within the department as a part of the organization, and who has direct responsibility for the activity. Documented procedures do not need to be lengthy and redundant. They should be simply written and easy to understand.

Procedures are an extension of the EMS manual (or its other controlling documentation) but are aimed at specific departments. As such, a particular procedure will outline an activity, or set of related activities, for one department (e.g., "Administration," "Mill"). Procedures are considered the second tier of documentation in the environmental management system.

■ TYPES OF PROCEDURES

There are two ways to write procedures: all-inclusive or as an "umbrella" document that points the way to work instructions.

All-inclusive procedures provide all the information an employee needs to know in completing a task. The umbrella procedure will direct the reader (employee, manager, or auditor) to one or more work instructions, or other reference documents that provide additional information needed to complete specific tasks for an activity.

An effective procedure will reduce the review needed for supervisors or auditors working in areas that they do not deal with on a regular basis, as activity responsibilities are clearly defined within the procedure.

If a procedure is solidly written, verification of an employee's performance is simply a matter of reading the description of the procedure and comparing it with the individual's actual performance. Detailed procedures will also provide guidance for employees, reducing the amount of training needed for new hires.

While procedures can incorporate detailed work instructions for employee use, they may become unwieldy and unattractive to an organization. Some procedures can cover three, five, or even more work instructions. For example, a procedure for chemical storage can deal with multiple chemicals, each requiring specific handling instructions. Use of an umbrella procedure in this instance would require nothing more than a half-page procedure that included an overview of chemical storage within a department; information on who is responsible for overseeing the storage; and a reference to the specific work instruction for each type of chemical covered.

It is best to consider the number of individual tasks an activity covers, and the amount of information needed for each individual work instruction, before choosing which type of procedure structure your organization needs. The choice may vary from department to department within the organization, and from activity to activity within the department. You can combine procedure styles within an environmental management system to meet the needs of the organization.

➤ **Writing the Procedure**

Procedures will cover each mandatory requirement, or "shall" of the ISO 14001 standard that applies to the specific departmental activity. The procedure should:

➤ Reference the department in which the procedure is used.

➤ Give a general description of the activity itself.

➤ Provide the title of the individual or individuals responsible for the activity.

➤ Outline when, where, and how the activity is performed.

➤ List, or make reference to standards that list the resources needed to perform the activity.

➤ Outline control measures for the activity.

➤ Make reference to standards or other criteria that may impact the activity (i.e., customer contract).

➤ If it is an "umbrella" procedure, make reference to specific work instruction(s) that guide the activity.

Umbrella procedures require individual work instructions. The reader of the procedure will find reference to the specific work instruction at the end of the umbrella procedure. Work instructions are directed at the doers of an organization—individuals carrying out activities covered by the environmental management system.

Where the umbrella procedure describes an activity in general and tells who is responsible for the activity, work instructions explain *how to* do the various tasks. Work instructions may target an individual employee or an entire department. They tell the operator what steps need to be followed to attain conformance with the organization's environmental policy and other requirements; what equipment and resources are required for a job, what precautionary measures need to be taken, and so forth.

The work instruction should be clearly labeled as to the procedure requiring the instruction. This is the documentation direction required by Section 4.4.4 of ISO 14000.

Work instructions contain specifics, and should be as detailed as necessary to assure clarity and compliance. Since work instructions are "how to" documents, they may change frequently.

➤ Writing the Work Instruction

As noted, a single procedure may cover multiple work instructions. The format of the work instructions will differ widely from department to department within the organization, and even from activity to activity within the department. Work instructions may be in the form of flowcharts, reporting forms, instruction cards, "travelers" (work vouchers), or contained in a detailed customer contract.

Look for existing material when developing instructions. Many documents probably exist and are currently in use within your organization. So the task for creating organizational EMS documentation will involve compiling a list of all tasks that fall under a certain activity, preparing a short procedure outlining the activity, naming the position responsible for the activity, and directing employees to the existing documents used to control task performance. The organization may wish to edit the current documents (which will become the work instructions) so they reference the procedure itself. This will create an easy-to-follow paper trail for any reader.

■ DOCUMENT CONTROL IN THE ENVIRONMENTAL MANAGEMENT SYSTEM

As you implement the environmental management system, it is vital to create and implement a document review process for verifying that the policy, manual, and procedures are in place and effective. For the purpose of ISO 14001 requirements, this is simply a means of managing the creation, approval, distribution, revision, storage, and disposal of the various types of documentation.

The ISO 14001 standard requires that current versions of relevant documents are available at all locations where activities critical to the effective operation of the environmental management system are conducted. Likewise, obsolete documents must be promptly removed from all points of issue and use.

Use common sense when determining how, and for how long, documents will be kept. All computer files and hard copy must be backed up for safety. As a protection against disaster, backup copies should be stored in a different location from that of the original. Length of storage time for documentation of any regulated activities is usually mandated. The organization must determine how long other documents will be kept and what, if any, records will be kept for historical use.

The organization should also be able to provide assurance that all documents are:

➤ Dated (including revision dates).

➤ Properly identified, clarifying what organization the document belongs to, along with the appropriate department, function, activity, and/or responsible position.

➤ Organized.

➤ Retained for a specified period of time.

Document control systems should be as simple and easy to operate as possible, and they should be sufficient to meet ISO 14000 requirements.

■ SETTING ENVIRONMENTAL OBJECTIVES AND TARGETS

Objectives are broad goals the organization has identified in its environmental policy to drive improved environmental performance. Targets are measurements of the objective and usually include a date by which implementation of the objective will be completed. If an organization is to achieve its objectives, associated targets must first be set and met. Targets assist management and auditors as a means of evaluating the organization's effectiveness in meeting their goals.

After an organization has established procedures for identifying the environmental aspects of its activities, products, and services that *have* or *can have* significant impacts on the environment and that it can control and influence, it can then rank the activities for the purpose of setting achievable environmental objectives.

Objectives and targets can have a broad application, extending across an entire organization, or they can be restricted to specific sites or activities.

➤ **Fundamentals of Setting Objectives**

Objectives are set once the organization has:

➤ Laid the foundation for setting specific objectives and targets in regard to the environmental policy.

➤ Determined the *actual* and *potential* impacts of activities, products, and/or services on the environment.

➤ Determined how well the site's operations conform to current legislation. Regulatory requirements must be considered when framing environmental objectives.

➤ Established which of these impacts needs to be controlled, reduced, or improved.

Based on the preceding information, management determines what needs to be done. This determination then becomes the organization's environmental objectives.

In determining environmental factors, consideration should be given to normal and abnormal operations within the organization, and to potential emergency conditions. Once these facts have been determined, organizations can work to prevent or minimize serious or irreversible environmental degradation through sound, scientifically based environmental management practices.

One criterion for setting environmental objectives is the significance of the impact. Environmental aspects must be assessed to determine which pose the greatest negative impact.

➤ The Four-Stage Plan for Setting Objectives

According to the ISO 14004 Environmental Management System guidance document, procedures for identifying and quantifying environmental aspects can be based on the following four-stage plan:

Stage 1. *Choose an activity or process to evaluate.*

Stage 2. *Identify as many environmental aspects associated with the selected activity or process as possible.* An organization that is evaluating a particular product would consider packaging, transportation, use, disposal, and so forth. (Alternatively, identification can be achieved by examining activities associated with each product or service that the organization provides.)

Stage 3. *Identify as many actual and potential, positive and negative, environmental impacts associated with each identified aspect as possible.* The disposal of a product could lead to the following impacts: wasted resources, landfill, litter, incineration, discharge to water, sewer, or air, smells, and so forth.

Stage 4. *Evaluate the significance of identified environmental impacts.* This will help the organization quantify its impacts and judgment. Overall cost criteria play a major roll in ranking and classifying environmental impacts, but consideration should also be given to:

Overall business management plans.

Scale of the impact.

Severity of the impact.

Probability of occurrence.

Permanence of the impact.

Concerns of interested parties.

Potential regulatory and legal exposure.

Difficulty of changing the impact.

Cost of changing the impact.

Effect of change on other activities and processes.

Effect on the public image of the organization.

Industry standards and goals.

Current technological options.

➤ Ranking Environmental Activities

After determining the significance of each aspect, the organization will be able to rank and prioritize them. The organization's management plan will be developed based on this ranking. Ranking will take into account:

1. Ability to eliminate or minimize the impacts.

2. Availability of appropriate resources needed to achieve item 1.

3. Special environmental concerns to consider based on the location of the facility *and* concerns of interested parties in the location.

4. Possible altering of environmental aspects and impacts by making changes to activities, products, or services.

5. Significance or severity of the potential environmental impact if a process fails.

6. Frequency of environmental impact.

7. Significance of environmental benefit in relation to the cost of the program.

8. Internal priorities.

9. Commitment to promote environmental awareness both internally and externally.

10. Time lines: short, intermediate, and long-term management plan objectives.

The Probable Risk Assessment Model (PRAM) is a good model for ranking aspects to determine impact significance. The model assigns numbers to attributes of the aspect such as probability, cost, and ability of the organization to control it. The sum total of each aspect's attributes can be ranked in a parieto diagram, and the organization can choose the aspects they wish to target.

Time lines and setting of multiple objectives with varying target dates are an important part of the continual improvement philosophy behind ISO 14001. While minimization of wastewater discharge and air emissions may both rank of prime importance, the time and money necessary to target the two objectives simultaneously may be prohibitive. However, one of these objectives could be chosen for immediate implementation along with lower ranking, but less time consuming and less costly, objectives. Time lines and evidence of multiple objectives with varying target dates will be an important part of the audit process.

Promotion of environmental awareness among employees may not rank as high as a significant impact like air emissions, but it is nonetheless valid. An objective might be to arrange an orientation program. By offering a training program, the organization can fulfill a short-term objective. Environmental awareness however, can create additional opportunities for the organization as empowered employees begin to identify new areas of environmental impact that the organization can control.

As stated earlier, objectives and targets can have a broad application, extending across an entire organization, or they can be restricted to specific sites or activities. Each objective and its targets should support the organization's environmental policy, and, wherever practicable, they should be specific and measurable. Plans for objectives and targets should take into account relevant findings from environmental reviews, identified environmental aspects, and their associated impacts and legal/regulatory requirements. If an organization desires to achieve an objective within a certain time period, a specific time frame can be assigned to that objective. The issue date and the target date establish the time frame for completion. If the objective is long-term, maybe even four or five years in length, multiple targets can be used for assessing the organization's accomplishments toward the final goal. For example, if an organization wished to create a new product made of 100 percent recycled materials and the targeted completion date was five years from today, targets could be set for initial research completion, prototype design, prototype testing, prototypes' rework, and a pilot marketing study.

Organizations should not be afraid of setting long-term objectives, as ISO 14001 is a dynamic system that is constructed specifically to address needed changes.

➤ Environmental Performance Indicators

One way objectives and targets can be quantified is through environmental performance indicators (EPIs). EPIs are measurable indicators, such as the level of air emissions, the percentage of waste recycled, and treatment system maintenance logs, that can be used to evaluate environmental performance.

By measuring an organization's environmental performance, objectives and targets can be tracked, and the organization can quantify, through measurable data, whether it is fulfilling its objectives and targets.

Inability or difficulty in quantifying an objective should not eliminate it from consideration under the ISO 14000 Environmental Management System. A utility company whose objective is to raise public awareness of energy use may choose to do quarterly newsletter mailings detailing peak hours and promoting energy use reduction. Their measurable target could be the number of newsletters mailed. However, it is impossible to verify that the newsletters have been read by the targeted audience. The objective, though difficult to quantify, is worthwhile.

A qualitative objective can also be worthwhile and acceptable. For example, numerous neighbors surrounding a composting operation sent the management letters complaining of the smell of the operation during the summer heat. The composting operation's objective is to reduce operational smell by adding newspaper to grass clippings with the intent of balancing the carbon to nitrogen ratio. The measurable target could be a phone call to all of the previous year's letter writers asking them to rank the level of the odor in the current year as compared to last year's. The "evaluation" of the new operational procedure is highly subjective, but is still valid.

Objectives and targets must be defined by appropriate levels of management, and must be periodically reviewed and revised. In setting objectives, remember that output should be dependent on input. If the measurable output (e.g., 30 percent reduction in emissions) is based on last year's level of emissions, and this year's product output rises by 40 percent, it would be virtually impossible to meet the objective set.

■ ENVIRONMENTAL MANAGEMENT PROGRAMS

For an organization to achieve its set objectives and targets, it must establish a strategic course of action. That is the purpose of the environmental management program as covered by Section 4.3.4 of the ISO 14001 standard.

The environmental management program is a *program of action*. It is an example of how environmental aspects and impacts may be addressed by an organization's environmental management system, and is a critical factor for ensuring its overall success.

The environmental management program may sound like a singular plan of action, but it generally consists of several different programs, running side by side, addressing all of the organization's impacts.

Each program addresses specific impacts of the organization's operations (processes, projects, products, services, sites, etc.) and has its own, unique objectives, priorities, time frame, and personnel. In following a long-term program, each accomplishment under the program would be considered a separate objective, meeting the ISO 14001 standard's requirement for continual improvement. Each department within an organization should have at least one environmental program to achieve.

Environmental management programs should be comprehensive, thorough, and based on hard data. Programs must clearly identify how objectives and targets are to be achieved and the time frame for their accomplishment so there is no room for misunderstanding.

Program objectives must be quantifiable in the form of indicators wherever possible, and defined with set time frames.

In terms of administering programs, responsibility and a clear line of communication must also be established at each level, and for each relevant function at any level. Responsibility needs to be assigned for every aspect of the program and necessary resources should be noted. Table 7-1 provides an example of an environmental management program.

Where appropriate and practical, environmental management programs should consider planning, marketing, disposal stages, design, and production.

If the program addresses a particular product, it should consider design, materials, use, production processes, and ultimate disposal.

If a program addresses installation or a significant change to a process, it should consider planning, design, construction, commissioning, operation and decommissioning

Setting and achieving environmental objectives in non-regulated areas is not the traditional approach for most

Table 7-1. An Environmental Management Program

(The following example is based on a coal-fired power plant that produces electricity and other forms of energy.)

Aspect	Burners.
Impact	Atmospheric emissions of air pollutants, per MI permit #1234.
Objective	To minimize, wherever fiscally and technologically possible, the release of nitrogen oxides into the atmosphere.
Target	To reduce the amount of nitrogen oxides that are emitted into the atmosphere, per unit of electricity generated, based on the levels measured in calender year 1996.
Indicator	Reduction of the 1996 level by 30 percent.
Current Environmental Performance	In calendar year 1996, the plant produced 41 thousand tons of nitrogen oxides. This amount was within regulatory limits. No formal notices or prosecutions were received.
Significant Environmental Impacts	Nitrogen oxide emissions, the use of natural resources, hazard waste disposal.
Action Plan	Replace three (3) coal burners with low nitrogen oxide burners. The new burners are projected to reduce nitrogen oxide emissions by 40 percent.
Assigned Responsibility	*John Brown* Title
Required Resources	$3 million to purchase the new burners. $80,000 to install the burners. 3 days training for operations staff. Installation of alternate technology, scrubbers, at a cost $6.8 million; projected operational costs: $278,000 per year.
Projected Date of Completion	January 1, 1998.

organizations, and may be a foreign concept to many operational managers. It is vital that top management clearly communicate the *intent* of ISO 14000 throughout the organization and give positive reinforcement of effective implementation. This may require use of a management training program to develop an understanding of the fundamentals of environmental management and the ISO 14000 standards; create awareness and perspective of the national and international environmental issues as they apply to the organization's operations and its corporate citizen's role; develop skills to build, implement, and maintain the system to achieve organizational objectives; and influence the integration of environmental ethics as a primary organizational management goal ensuring its place in the decision-making process.

The education process should present a realistic picture of where the organization is today, where the industry as a whole stands today, and where the organization would like to be. The program should establish the environmental personality of the organization and present a broad picture of environmental science needed to take the organization forward. No change in environmental behavior—of the management or the organization—will occur unless there is a change in environmental attitude.

In the process of implementation, some organizations may need to revamp their current incentive program to facilitate the process. For example, one cleaning chemical may have a lower purchase price than another. If an operational manager's incentives are based on that cost alone, other factors impacting the organization and its resources may be overlooked in making the purchase. Such factors could include careful control requirements for unstable or caustic chemicals; handling requirements necessitating special employee training; and need to establish special emergency response procedures to deal with spills or accidents. Purchase price alone is an invalid measurement, as hidden costs are an organizational impact that would be excluded from the incentive formula.

If an activity or product is new or modified, the program should include an environmental review. The program should also cover all appropriate environmental objectives and targets; the personnel responsible for overseeing each stage; and the procedures necessary for reviewing and controlling the changes.

Environmental management programs need to be revised periodically to ensure that any changes made to objectives or targets are incorporated.

Nobody knows an organization like its employees—from CEO to janitorial staff. Communicate the organization's intent to the employees and allow them to provide input for identification of areas that can be controlled by the environmental management system. Departmental teams are an excellent means of brainstorming possibilities of minimizing environmental impact within a departmental area. Process improvement teams are an excellent way of integrating and prioritizing departmental objectives and ensuring full organizational involvement. Employees care.

Review every department. Environmental awareness is the key to managing resource use and misuse; each costs money and has environmental impact. With little or no effort, big savings can be realized by targeting areas outside those organizational areas currently identified as environmental (regulatory). Encourage creative thinking. Regulation activities may be a part of ISO 14000, but control of these activities alone does not fulfill the intent of the standards. Apply the concept of environmental aspects broadly—interdepartmental, community, regional, or even global. Remember that environmental consciousness must be learned, but in time it becomes an automatic operational skill that requires little effort. Simply:

➤ *Ask questions.* Talk to knowledgeable suppliers, supporting agencies such as Extension Service, professional organizations, and peers.

➤ *Read labels and manufacturer's information sheets.* Evaluate products before making purchases of organizational supplies (paper, cleaning supplies, inks and markers, etc.).

➤ *Keep abreast of changes.* Research advances in technology and industry operations that can help control environmental impact.

➤ *Search for substitutes.* Just as the newer aqueous cleaning processes in manufacturing are less toxic than traditional acid processes, many supplies used on a daily basis can be replaced by more "earth-friendly" substitutes. Look for vegetable-based inks (rather than alcohol-based), papers utilizing recycled fibers, and whenever possible, cleaning supplies that do not use chlorine or other toxic bases.

➤ *Think "environmental impact."* Form partnerships with high-quality environmental education programs like Projects WET (Water Education for Teachers) and Learning Tree to provide affordable, sound, scientifically based, educational support of schools and nonprofit organizations.

➤ *Get involved.* Encourage employee volunteerism for one or more annual community environmental projects chosen and promoted as an integral part of the organization's environmental management system.

➤ *Empower employees.* Ask them to step forward to work on department committees, head individual organization action projects such as recycling, and provide useful tips in organization suggestion boxes.

As the environmental management system will require new procedures and programs for implementation, employees must be properly prepared to implement and maintain it.

Management must ensure that employees, especially those carrying out environmental management functions, understand the system, are competent to perform their duties in conformance with the environmental policy, and understand the consequences that can result when operating procedures are not followed. Failure to provide necessary support means failure of the system. Therefore, management has to determine the level of experience, competence, and training required for personnel at different levels and with different functions.

In determining the training required for implementation and maintenance of the environmental management system, management should emphasize the skills and methods required to carry out specific tasks competently. Training should stress the higher levels of participation and self-direction that employees working within the system have in environmental activities. Employees need to understand and appreciate the environmental benefits that can be derived from improved personal performance.

Awareness of the intent of ISO 14000, awareness of environmental issues, and interest in changes within the organization's industry must be fostered. This will go far to enlist employees' support and commitment. Typical training methods include workshops and seminars, lectures, case studies, videos, and practical demonstrations.

■ SYSTEM CHANGES

Changes to documented procedures will be required from time to time. Forces dictating system changes may be external or internal. Some examples of external forces include:

➤ Changes or updates in the ISO 14001 standards.

➤ Changes in governmental regulations.

➤ Focus of public issues or concerns.

Internal changes that may initiate change include:

➤ Inclusion of new environmental objective areas in the organization's management plan.

➤ Organizational growth, new areas of operation, or changes in operations.

➤ Revision of newly designed system procedures as they are evaluated for effectiveness.

➤ Corrective and preventive actions.

Interrelationship diagram models displaying cause-and-effect relations of a central issue are an integral part of establishing and verifying procedures. Critical issues will have an unusually high number of relationships. Procedures control the relationships.

Because the ISO 14001 standard requires continual improvement in environmental performance, it is important to verify the effectiveness of procedures and of procedural changes implemented to correct nonconformities. Verification can be accomplished by showing consistency of results;

prevention of occurrence; ability to detect, provide feedback, and correct; and ability to identify. For example, determining the effectiveness of emission and discharge controls measured by monitoring activities can be difficult, as the organization must analyze large amounts of data, over long- and/or short-term periods. Peak period readings may appear vastly out of line with readings from other points in time. Assemblage of data in a scattergram is an effective means of analyzing data. Data in scattergrams present consistent, graphic patterns of data ranges that can be clearly discerned by all interested parties.

Many have pointed out the inherent paradox in defining highly specific procedures for individual behavior and, at the same time, encouraging those individuals to be creative problem solvers. One can negate the other, or enhance it. It is a matter of management perspective.

The beauty of a systems approach is that it forces us to define and control the momentum of an operation. To develop a procedure is really to give it intense individual attention and to see how it can be controlled within the context of an entire operation. If the individual is encouraged and trained to look at these details from the perspective of improving them, then defined procedures can also lead to significant innovations.

A systemic approach need not be an uncreative one. What a system does is to force the participants to look at all aspects of their effort, to overlook nothing. And looking at a problem from multiple perspectives is the essence of non-linear, creative thinking.

Managers need to look at each environmental procedure through the eyes of not only the businessperson, but the engineer, the accountant, the production supervisor, the federal regulator, the ISO 14001 auditor and, ultimately, the customer. As one environmental manager put it, "A system forces you to split your personality into so many perspectives that it's like having a committee meeting in your head."

While procedures must be highly specific, they can also inspire people to see the possibilities for new, more innovative procedures. They can inspire continual improvement. They can if—and it's a big "if"—each employee feels he or she has the opportunity to express ideas, and to make a difference.

Essential to any truly useful system is its ability to adapt and change as new knowledge and improvement opportunities dictate. Karl von Clausewitz, a Prussian general, wrote a hundred and fifty years ago: "I do not expect a plan to survive beyond the first contact with the enemy. Strategy is not a lengthy action-plan. It is the evolution of a central idea through continually changing circumstances."

If you incorporate the idea of continual improvement into the way your people think, environmental procedures will be the stepping-stones to evolution.

Avoiding the Pitfalls

Having each some shingles of thought well dried, we sat and whittled them.

—HENRY DAVID THOREAU

As you put together an environmental management system, your goal should be to construct it so that it passes any audit, internal or external. Be aware, however, that continual fine-tuning of your initial ISO 14001 environmental management system is going to be a fact of life. The EMS is *expected* to change. That's how you realize one of its primary commitments—continual improvement.

Repeatedly, you'll find the value of "Say what you do. Do what you say. And prove it." Keep thinking of this as you add the EMS to your existing management system. It will help you to reach your goals of successful ISO 14001 implementation, certification, and sustainability.

Your company's ISO 14001 EMS may look entirely different from that of an associate's firm. Yet they may both be in total conformity with all requirements of the standard. Your goal should be to adapt ISO 14001 to your existing management system and environmental management program. You want to weave the EMS right into the fiber of your current operational structure. You should build on what you have, rather than tossing it all and starting from scratch. The system must meet your needs.

As noted earlier, if you've already brought in the ISO 9000 quality management system, you're accustomed to systems development. ISO 14000 simply changes the focus from quality of your product to the environmentally conscious management of your organization.

■ PLANNING EQUALS COMMON SENSE

The process may at times be complex and involve multiple levels and efforts, but in the end, it's all really common sense. The ISO 14001 EMS system requires the same managment principles that must be incorporated for any major undertaking to work effectively and realize its purpose. Whether you're organizing a charity fundraiser, forming a company golf league, or planning a new product line for one of the Big Three automakers, you must use a systemic approach to manage and monitor the process. That approach doesn't appear out of the sky one day, all nice and neat. There are steps and stops along the way. At each check point, from the very first, you should answer these questions.

In deciding on the project:

➤ What are we trying to accomplish?

➤ Why are we doing it?

➤ How are we going to do it?

➤ How much are we going to spend doing it?

➤ When are we going to do it?

➤ What else do we need to consider?

Then, once the project is conceptualized:

➤ Who's going to be accountable for the success of the project?

➤ Where will it be implemented and managed from?

➤ How will it be implemented—what are the key steps and required resources?

➤ When must the project be completed?

➤ In what other ways can our achievements benefit us (i.e., marketing)?

Answering these questions gives you a basic design. The project is now rolling, but to make sure you reach your goal you need to determine:

➤ How will we track the progress of the project?

➤ How will we track costs?

➤ How will we know it's being done right?

➤ What will we do if it isn't?

It's these same "who, what, where, when, why, and how" questions that are ingrained in student journalists. These very questions must be asked and then answered to conform with ISO 14001 requirements of policy, planning, implementation/operation, checking and correction action, and management review. You start with the first question, work your way through to the last, and then begin again. That's the ISO 14001 EMS action cycle.

Development and implementation of an ISO 14001-conformant EMS is a significant project. Once implemented, maintenance requires a systematic, continuing, repetitive process geared toward refinement, revision, and improvement—just like other management systems in any ongoing, successful business. This consistent quality assurance objective is called "continual improvement" in ISO 14001. The goal is for your company to improve the way its products, services, and processes affect the environment.

First and last, ISO 14001 is a management system. It is not an environmental compliance program. Mixing the two concepts within your 14001 system could lead to trouble.

The success of an ISO 14000 environmental management system's goals and objectives requires complete commitment and involvement of *every* employee. When properly implemented, the ISO 14001 EMS Specification (the only part of the ISO 14000 standard against which an organization is audited) provides the framework necessary to achieve this key commitment.

■ DON'T REINVENT THE WHEEL

How you apply this framework to your particular organization, and how you fit ISO 14000 to your existing structure, is left up to you. Don't try doing the reverse. Don't try molding your organization to fit ISO 14000. Integrating ISO 14000 into your existing structure is the intention of the standard, and from our implementation expert and auditor resources, we learn this is really the best way to approach it.

Ralph Grover, President of Environomics Risk Group, Ltd., an environmental consulting firm, is an expert in environmental management systems, both inside, from an implementation point of view, as well as outside, from the perspective of a third-party EMS auditor. He reports, "I'm convinced more money is spent fitting the existing system to 14001 than in fitting 14001 to the present system. Besides causing too much organizational disruption, the expense factor truly jeopardizes the survival of the EMS implementation effort. In any organization there are cost issues. If you try to fit the existing system to ISO 14001 and, as a result, you go over budget, implementation will be dead. It's best to fit ISO 14001 to your management system."

He explains, "Bringing in ISO 14001 requires a heartier sell-job than ISO 9000, the quality management system standard. Why? Simply because the corporate culture sees quality as related to the customer who buys the product/service. This is the organization's direct source of revenue. Environmental management is still seen by many as belonging on the expense side of the ledger. The contrary is true; it's actually an indirect producer of income.

"It's much like the different ways a company views sales versus public relations. With sales, the result is obvious, often immediate, but definitely direct. With public relations, it takes longer and is more difficult initially to see how this helps the bottom line. So the less disruption and expense associated with ISO 14001 implementation, the better are the chances for the idea to get airborne."

How your company shapes its ISO 14001 environmental management system depends on the organization's type, management style, size, location(s), number and types of regulatory permits, resources, market makeup and requirements, scope and status of current environmental management efforts, technological sophistication, and many other factors. There is a common thread linking the experiences of 14000 experts and those who've completed the process of implementing a 14000 system. To have a fully functioning EMS that will pass even the toughest third-party certification audit, you must have commitment, integration, and supervision.

➤ Top Management Commitment

This must be present from the onset of initial planning and remain throughout the implementation cycle of the EMS, including assignment of the required level of resources needed to plan, develop, implement, monitor, and improve your environmental program. The drafters of ISO 14001 wrote provisions of resources into the standard because they knew that, without it, the EMS would crumble. There will be no foundation to keep it standing, or any assigned priority to keep it working. In the ISO 14001 system, accountability starts and ends with top management.

➤ EMS Integration throughout the Organizational Structure

Your ISO 14001 environmental management system, and its assigned targets, must become as important to those inside your company's walls as to the integrity of the environment it is intended to protect. Employees, from the top of the organizational chart to the bottom, must connect the EMS to their job responsibilities and be evaluated for the part they play in its success. Environmental management must be integrated vertically and horizontally to keep the EMS wheel turning down, around, up . . . down, around, up . . . .

Get everyone on track right at the beginning and make sure they feel part of the solution. Reward positive EMS efforts, big and small.

➤ Environmental Management System Supervision

Call it follow-through. As in nearly any sport, the desired result happens when the necessary action is completed. Individuals, companies, and governments remain successful if they do what they say they're going to do. "Say what you do. Do what you say. Prove it," is the protocol necessary for an effective EMS. To have that protocol, you must have checkpoints along the line to keep things moving. If a deadline is set, make sure procedures call for routine and regular progress updates. That's follow-through. There may be a temptation to reduce supervision of the EMS, postpone target dates, or minimize setting new objectives once you've passed your EMS audit or have reached those first goals. Don't let this happen. Correctly implementing ISO 14001 includes the commitment to continual improvement. This means maintaining vigil over its effective functioning. Routine EMS audits, either internal or external, provide objective verification of your vigilance.

The difference top-management support makes is also one of the reasons the ISO 14000 environmental management system shows such promise. Confirmation of this fact comes from Joseph Koretsky, Manager of LCD Quality Assurance for Sharp Microelectronics Tech, and an experienced environmental auditor. As an auditor, he has seen the results of weak upper-management commitment. While in charge of implementing ISO 14001 for his own firm, Koretsky soon realized the value of his company president's vocal backing of the EMS.

Koretsky reports, "I believe the weakest link (in implementation) is the lack of commitment on the part of management. This is primarily driven by the lack of understanding of what an EMS is, and what the implication is of implementing a company-wide EMS program. Historically, environmental issues were handled by a specialist who was usually buried in the bowels of the organization. No one wanted to hear about these issues since they were perceived as not contributing to the bottom line. Line management was so focused on their primary functions that the less they heard from the environmental people, the better. If there was a problem, the approach was to find the easiest, cheapest, and most expeditious fix. Getting at the root cause was not a motivation."

Koretsky continues, "Suddenly ISO 14000 arrives and is becoming a popular buzz-word. Many companies are wanting to jump on the bandwagon. However, they have no idea what this implies. The conventional wisdom is that the environmental person will be able to do what is required in his spare time, and that miraculously, they will get registration with a minimal investment. Since there is no understanding, there is no commitment throughout the organization. The people who have to implement the system have no desire to do it, and there is no direction from management to do it either."

He tells us the inevitable result, "This approach is certain to fail and significantly increase everyone's level of frustration, and will taint future environmental improvement efforts. I believe that, before a company embarks on this program, the top management has to fully understand the scope of the EMS activities and be willing to support them with time, money and resources. . . . Management has to walk the talk. They must demonstrate by actions, not words, that they are committed. This is a site-wide activity that everyone must participate in. A good way of selling the program is to try to quantify the potential cost savings realized by implementing ISO 14001."

The process went quite differently when ISO 14001 was implemented at Sharp Microelectronics. This was in part due to lessons learned during the company's ISO 90002 implementation/certification experience.

Koretsky describes his boss's approach, "Jon Shroyer is the president of Sharp Microelectronics Technology (SMT), a high tech facility in Camas, Washington. We manufacture LCD panels for laptop and portable computers, design and manufacture IC device products and do research and development of personal communications devices, LSI process development, and LCD process development. In addition, SMT is the landlord to two other Sharp subsidiaries which are responsible for sales (Sharp Electronics Corporation) and research and development in the field of multimedia (Sharp Laboratories of America). Jon is very committed to the value of both a quality-management and environmental-management system and has made his commitment clear to the entire site. The chief executives of the other two companies . . . are equally committed. Jon recognized the need for a clear message of management commitment during the ISO 9002 registration activities in 1993. He and his staff (the executive Operating Committee) stressed the importance of ISO 9000 during staff and area meetings."

According to Koretsky, Shroyer made clear to everyone management's commitment to the ISO 9000 quality management system. He defines management "walking the talk" in this way: "By this I mean that their actions were much more important than their words. [They knew] employees would be scrutinizing their actions to determine the level of commitment. Jon made it clear to everyone that the Quality Management Manager (who became the ISO 9000 management representative) had his complete support, and that the management representative spoke for the entire senior management team. The successful ISO 9000 registration was due in large part to this support. It made the very difficult task easier because there was a minimum of escalations required to resolve issues."

Shortly after the company earned ISO 9002 registration, Shroyer began studying the ISO 14000 environmental management system, and he followed the same pattern for his ISO 14000 implementation. Says Koretsky, "Jon has been very active during the entire program. . . . As with ISO 9000, he has been very vocal to employees in his support for the program. He has reviewed the overall program schedule and insists on regular progress reports and is always available to provide the necessary support. . . . He is firmly committed to this program, and everyone knows this is fact. Therefore, I have to use the hammer very little. I can't overemphasize the importance of management commitment."

Chapter

The Internal Audit

The very purpose of existence is to reconcile the glow-
ing opinion we have of ourselves with the appalling
things that others think about us.

—QUENTIN CRISP

Your environmental management system is in place, up and running. You have a few months' worth of records generated, your monitoring equipment has had the bugs worked out, your people (and your vendors' on-site people) have been trained, manuals have been printed and distributed, signage is in place, and you have procedures worked out and implemented for every environmentally sensitive activity that you and your EMS team could identify in your facility.

Great! Do you phone the registrar and make an appointment for a registration audit?

Not yet.

A test pilot doesn't take an unproven aircraft up for its first flight until it has passed a rigorous series of tests to determine if it is ready for such an endeavor. And you cannot expose your company to the time, expense, and scrutiny of a registration audit until you have first determined its readiness through your own examination—a *first-party* or *internal* audit.

Internal audits can provide three principal benefits to your company:

1. They can uncover nonconformities that might cause your company to fail in an actual registration audit.

2. They act as "dress rehearsals" that prepare you, your company, and your employees for the registration audit.

3. *If* a registrar has thoroughly examined your internal-audit records as part of its initial review process, and *if* the registrar is completely satisfied with the credentials of your internal-audit team and the methods by which the internal audit was performed, then the registrar *may* elect to conduct a less exhaustive (and less expensive) audit of your site, using a smaller audit team than it might otherwise have selected: If you are thoroughly prepared, it can save you time and money in the registration audit (but remember, this is the registrar's *option*—it is not a requirement).

■ THE INTERNAL TEAM

Internal teams are usually a kinder, gentler approach to getting your organization accustomed to having its EMS examined. It's one thing to have a stranger walking around your foundry with a clipboard; it's another when it's Joe from Assembly, the same guy everybody sees every year at the Christmas party.

This lower level of formality (the opening-meeting statement might go something like, "We're gonna take a look at the training records and see if instructions have been posted where needed—wanna have lunch when we're done?") helps get your operation used to having its EMS examined, and what may have been a disruption and a stressor quickly becomes just another part of doing business.

Training some of your people as auditors, and then using them to audit several operations or facilities, can be a real cost-saver. Even after you have factored in training costs, expenses, benefits, and salaries, internal auditors can, in the long run, prove to be less expensive than bringing in outside people for preliminary audits.

One big plus is that internal auditors are your own people, bound by no proprietary-information disclosure rules, and faced with no conflict of interest if they tell you how to fix a nonconformity. As your in-house expert, an internal auditor can be a valuable resource in tightening and improving your EMS.

■ SELECTING YOUR AUDITOR CANDIDATES

The people you select for internal-auditor training can come from just about any part of your company. Give preference to individuals with environmental education and experience, but those whom you designate as internal auditors should also possess certain personal attributes that will help them navigate the (for the moment, at least) relatively uncharted waters of EMS auditing. They should be:

Diplomatic

Professional

Articulate

Judicious

Communicative

Honest

Unbiased

Inquiring

Observant

Understanding

Industrious

Fair-minded

Thick-skinned

The auditor candidate must understand that an audit is not a search-and-destroy expedition. He or she will be evaluating a process, not the operators of that process. But will the co-workers who must answer probing questions be equally well-informed? The fact that auditor and auditee are already acquainted contributes to the informality of the internal audit process. It does not, however, detract from the objective precision with which that audit must be performed.

Since an internal auditor will, in effect, become an internal "ambassador" of your company, visiting people throughout the operation, there are also some "red flags" that may disqualify an individual for this duty, however astute the person may be about environmental issues. An internal auditor should *not:*

➤ Display negativity.

➤ Criticize.

➤ Get sidetracked.

➤ Argue.

➤ Compare the auditee with others.

➤ Discuss company policies.

These negative traits should be obvious, but can be easy to overlook when searching for an environmentally savvy individual within your workforce. Be especially careful to choose people with a professional demeanor—you'll save yourself regrets in the long run.

You also want to avoid auditing a department by a person who is internal to any of its operations. You may think this is a precaution to avoid "the fox guarding the henhouse," and certainly that factors into this precaution. But it's not the main reason; most employees genuinely want their organizations to be as environmentally friendly as possible.

The main reason for auditing with people not intimate to an operation is the "train-track syndrome." People who live next to train tracks rarely notice the train passing. Why? Because it's happened so often that they no longer view it as unusual.

The same thing can happen in a department or a facility. The people who are there every day may get so used to a situation (such as lack of documentation on an emergency procedure that "everybody knows") they will fail to note it as an observation or a nonconformity.

■ PROVIDING TRAINING FOR INTERNAL AUDITORS

Training for your people is available from several sources. The best, in my estimation, comes from organizations that also provide EMS training and ISO 14000 Lead Auditor training.

Good training does more than teach people to rote memorize the ISO 14001 criteria. It also teaches them to think creatively, investigate objectively, and use evidence-based criteria for their judgments.

Denise Seipke and Ralph Grover, ISO 14000 Lead Auditor seminar instructors for Perry Johnson, Inc., teach their seminar attendees to take a fresh look at familiar situations by asking them to think of potential environmental impacts for a completely fictitious company, XYZ Power Company.

Denise and Ralph begin by presenting the following thumbnail sketch of XYZ, which they describe as "a very progressive" utility company:

➤ The company's main business is the generation of electrical power.

➤ The power is turbine-generated and distributed to customers via a conventional electrical power grid.

. . . (So far, so good, but at this point, XYZ begins to seem a little weird). . . .

➤ The energy source used to turn the turbines is *squirrels*—millions of squirrels running around in little exercise wheels.

➤ The squirrels are fed cheese, which drops from a hopper and is brought to each squirrel via conveyer line.

➤ A local river is tapped as a freshwater source for the squirrels.

➤ Liquid and solid wastes are dropped through a mesh grid, collected, and buried in a landfill.

➤ Since the squirrels *do* breathe, fresh air is continuously brought into the generating plant via powered air intakes, and stale air is exhausted through chimneys.

That, briefly, is the state of XYZ power. In the seminar, once they have stopped laughing, auditor candidates postulate possible environmental impacts for XYZ Power; and role-playing as internal auditors, they also look for possibilities for continual improvement of the plant's environmental posture.

Here are some of the potential environmental impacts brought up by a typical Perry Johnson, Inc., seminar group.

➤ Air Concerns

These would affect neighbors both near and far. Since fresh air is continuously being brought in, and waste air exhausted, there is a high probability that odors—from the squirrels, from their wastes, and from the cheese with which they are fed—will be noticeable throughout both the plant and the surrounding countryside. How much of the waste air is being exhausted per hour or day, and how do we know (is the measuring equipment calibrated)?

In addition, old cheese and waste may become breeding grounds for molds and bacteria, creating a potential biohazard for workers in the plant and neighbors downwind of the plant.

What about airborne impacts associated with the squirrels themselves? Squirrels are living, breathing organisms and could potentially spread viruses and other communicable diseases to both humans (inside the plant and out) and other domestic animals. Because we have literally *millions* of squirrels here, there is also going to be a certain mortality rate, and we have to consider what method will be used for the detection of dead squirrels and the disposal of their carcasses.

What about allergies? Some people are allergic to animal dander; presumably such people would be climbing the walls if the dander from a million rodents were to be carried their way by the wind. And the same goes for parasites carried by the squirrels: If any of those can become airborne, another potential biohazard exists.

Finally, anyone who has ever walked in the woods has probably heard a squirrel chattering. Millions of squirrels chattering would probably be a significant source of noise pollution. So would the sounds of millions of exercise wheels squeaking, all at the same time.

➤ Water Concerns

Millions of squirrels would consume a prodigious amount of water. Exactly how much freshwater does the plant consume each day? Is there equipment to measure this? Is it calibrated? Is the river capable of sustaining the continual drawdown? At what point does the drawdown begin to affect downstream neighbors? Does the plant have this point targeted, and does it have a workable plan (i.e., trucking in water from another, larger freshwater source), in the event that critical river levels are reached?

What about liquid wastes? Those aren't going into the landfill, are they? How are the wastes being treated? Is recycling in place to restore freshwater levels in the freshwater source? In that case, how much recycling is done (remember, such things must be targeted). What steps are being taken to prevent possible aquifer incursion from solid waste and dead squirrels?

Do squirrels carry waterborne viruses and other diseases that can be transmitted through drinking water? How does the plant know whether such things are being carried out in the wastewater? Again, is there measuring equipment, and is it calibrated? Is there some type of filtration or biotreatment in place to prevent such an impact? Are emergency measures in place to prevent biological catastrophe if this treatment plant goes down? Has the necessary training been provided to employees and on-site vendors, and are instructions readily available?

➤ Land Concerns

The landfill use should be a point of concern with XYZ: What is the company doing to keep landfill use to a minimum, and what measures are in place to produce continual improvements in this aspect? Again, we will need measurement (scales weighing the trucks that haul waste away), the measuring devices (scales) will need to be calibrated regularly, accurate records should be kept. And there should be targets in place so fluctuations will trigger investigations or alarms.

Any time you have high concentrations of livestock, animal escapes and any resulting feral populations will become a concern. Are the squirrels of a species native to the area, or would an escape create an introduced species or (through interbreeding with native squirrels) subspecies? Are steps in place to prevent escapes? Do the employees most closely associated with squirrelkeeping have the necessary training in such steps, and are instructions conspicuously posted in the work areas most likely to be affected? Has management exercised due care to prevent feral populations (i.e., spaying and neutering of the plant's squirrels)? Is food use monitored so wastage can be minimized and efficiencies can be noted and exploited (management by exception)? Is the equipment used for such measurement calibrated? Are the records of food use, waste output, and so forth, readily available to those who need them?

➤ Other Concerns

So far, most of what we're investigating concerns the power source for the plant. But there are other aspects, as well. How about the bearings on the exercise wheels? Are they quiet (in-plant noise pollution), efficient (reduction of energy use), and durable (reduction of scrap)? Are the generators of an efficient design? Is the power grid effective and designed for minimal environmental impact? How does the plant measure power output; how is the measuring equipment calibrated and where are the records kept? Is output continually compared with raw-material use, to note waste and efficiencies?

XYZ will either have its own dairy farms or a vendor to supply the cheese food-source for the squirrels. Are the dairy cattle of a low- or nonpolluting variety? Are the environmental aspects of the dairy farm being properly considered and controlled?

This list of potential aspects and impacts for XYZ Power Company could go on and on (and proceed from the sublime to the ridiculous). But through this exercise, audit seminar attendees learn to use logic and intuitive questioning to uncover potential environmental aspects, to learn where measurement and record-keeping are necessary, and to detect potential nonconformances.

Concerns of animal rights activists (external parties) must be considered under ISO 14001 when setting objectives and targets for XYZ Power Co.

➤ Areas for Improvement and Means of Improvement

Were the auditors a third-party team performing a registration audit, their work would now be done. But a critical difference between the formal, registration audit and an informal, internal audit is that the company's own audit team may, and in most cases should, provide suggestions for the improvement of the plant and its potential environmental aspects, as there is no conflict of interest when the auditors are your own employees.

Some of the improvements typically suggested for XYZ Power by seminar attendees include:

➤ Targeting squirrel age and performance to keep the squirrel population at most efficient levels.

➤ Using several varieties of squirrels and noting (management by exception) the most efficient species, so it can become the dominant species used in the power-generation process.

➤ Discontinuing the use of cheese as a food-source and substituting a more appropriate and natural food for the squirrels (nuts and seeds).

➤ Recycling dead squirrels into the fur industry.

➤ Experimenting with the use of low-friction bearings on turbine wheels and noting (management by exception) the most efficient varieties; this can be a continual process, as newer and more efficient bearings become available.

➤ Repatriation of elderly squirrels to forest areas in which they might become a useful part of the ecosystem (another form of recycling).

➤ Composting waste materials, rather than consuming landfill space.

➤ Recycling worn-out wheels and cages as reusable scrap metal.

➤ Planting noise- and odor-buffer "green belts" around the plant site to minimize impacts on neighboring residences, businesses, and communities or building of artificial wetlands for animal waste management.

And eventually, right around this point in the seminar, somebody *finally* speaks up and says, "You know, there has to be a more efficient method of generating electricity then putting squirrels in cages and having them turn turbines. Maybe XYZ should be using something less costly and complicated—hydro- or wind-power—instead."

XYZ now becomes a more common and efficient (if less thought-provoking) type of energy company. . . .

There are courses for internal auditors and courses for lead auditors conducting third-party audits. At least some of your people should take the latter, as it teaches them what to expect of an outside auditing party and (more importantly) how to think like an outside auditing party. Auditors who know how certification audits run will also be able to groom your people for the experience and assure a smooth-running and efficient audit when the outside team comes in.

■ ADVICE FOR INTERNAL AUDITORS

Their coursework should teach them this, but just to make sure, coach your internal auditors on the following effective investigative techniques.

When interviewing, remember that how you ask questions determines in large part the answers you will receive. It is essential, out of respect for the interviewed party's time, that you plan ahead. Decide the scope of your questions and the amount of time needed. Remember that the people you will interview are unlikely to be as familiar as you are with the reason for the audit or the nature of management-system models.

Keep your questions simple. Don't just rephrase, in question form, an element of the standard against which you're auditing. Instead, create an atmosphere of trust and communication. Be sincere in your inquiries if you expect to obtain the information you need.

Talk to employees, from machine operator to clerk, with the intention of finding out what they do, not whether they're doing it correctly. Speak their language. Show respect for the workers' level of knowledge and expertise about their job function. Stress also that you are there to audit the environmental management system, not people's performance.

To get the most information possible, ask open-ended questions. Give an operator the opportunity to explain as much as possible about his or her job. Questions starting with words like "who," "what," "when," "where" and "how" are likely to garner much more information than questions that can be answered with a simple "yes" or "no."

Asking an operator to demonstrate their job for you, showing a genuine interest and curiosity on your part, will elicit a wealth of information and may even prompt additional questions. People love to talk about their work. If you're sincerely interested, and it shows, you will have established exactly the kind of rapport needed to obtain the information you want and need.

One last piece of advice on interviewing during an audit: Question the person who actually changes the filter, files the documents, conducts the training, and so forth. Don't undermine workers' competence, or your own credibility, by going above their heads and talking to supervisors. A supervisor is not likely to be as good a source of information as the person who has firsthand contact with a particular task on a daily basis.

■ REAL VERSUS "UNREAL"

Nonconformities uncovered during an internal audit should be treated (and rectified) with the same seriousness and thoroughness that you would show to a nonconformity uncovered by a third-party team: *Regardless of who found it, a nonconformity is a nonconformity.* And every nonconformity is detrimental to your EMS. The object here is not to get a certificate; it is to create a system that helps you manage and diminish your operation's environmental impacts. The ISO 14000 certificate simply states there is objective evidence that the system does this.

■ THE VALUE OF INTERNAL AUDITORS

People sometimes think of company audit teams, or internal auditors, as the second string of the auditing world. I would vigorously dispute that allegation.

A third-party (registrar-provided) audit team needs to be able to spot potential nonconformities and gauge their relative impact (i.e., whether they are major or minor). It also needs to be astute enough to make observations of situations that may not be nonconformities, but could trigger one unless corrected.

That takes training and experience. A company's internal auditors must do all that and should also be able to suggest appropriate actions to fix nonconformities, actions that will satisfy a registrar's inquiry.

The auditors dispatched by the registrar need only the ability to spot what's broken, and to later see if it has, indeed, been remedied. You can liken it to a customer taking a warranted car into a dealership—the customer only needs the ability to say, "It's not driving right." It's up to the mechanic (the company being audited) to fix the car to the customer's satisfaction. The customer needn't know anything about repairing a car; all this person needs is the ability to recognize when it's running right.

But the first question an internal auditor is liable to get about a nonconformity is, "Well, how do we fix it?" And the internal auditor who can provide a workable answer to that question is of great value to the company.

While external auditors need fairly detailed knowledge of the industry being audited, they don't necessarily need the diagnostic skills and ability to "think outside the box" that are required of an internal auditor. So here's an important tip to managers: Don't think of your internal auditors as second-class citizens. They may be the most important resource you have as you get ready for your registration audit.

The Registration Audit

We judge ourselves by what we feel capable of doing,
while others judge us by what we have already done.

—Henry Wadsworth Longfellow

W hile you're investigating the idea of implementing ISO 14000, part of your consideration should
include whether or not you plan to seek formal
registration/certification to the ISO 14001 standard.

This is your decision. We have reviewed the many benefits this environmental management system will bring your
organization. Becoming registered to the standard is the best
way for you to maximize your implementation efforts. You
could claim you have an effectively functioning EMS, and
are doing your utmost to protect and preserve the environment. But how will you prove it ? An ISO 14001 registration
certificate is proof.

Some of your customers may require ISO 14001 registration in their contracts. This is already the case in European Union (EU) markets. Your environmental risk/liability insurance carrier might also strongly suggest it. Your banker may start asking you about ISO 14000. You really don't want to be put on the defensive in any of these cases. Scrambling to implement ISO 14000 and then rushing registration will prove draining and may not result in a certificate. It's quite possible this method could increase costs in both the implementation and registration phases.

Some companies implement ISO 14000 with no immediate goal of seeking formal certification/registration to the standard. At a later date, they decide to go ahead and complete the certification process. Our consultants have often heard this approach from companies: "We'll develop ISO 14000 as a system for the internal enhancement of our existing environmental program. We'll live with it for a while before seeking registration. We'll get it in place and see what it does."

For some entities, this may be a good decision, especially if they have other priorities related to their size, type of product or service, customer base, or financial status. There's no denying this is a much better method than rushing too quickly through implementation on to registration.

Whether you decide at the start that your goal is ISO 14000 registration, or you decide to apply for it later, you need to know all the steps involved in the process, including answers to these questions:

➤ What's involved in the process?

➤ Who determines how the ISO 14001 registration process is conducted?

➤ How long does it take?

➤ Whom do I contact if ISO 14001 registration is my goal?

➤ How do I know they are qualified?

➤ How much does ISO 14001 certification cost?

Answers to some of these questions will be clear-cut. Others depend on many factors such as the scope of your ISO 14000 EMS; how many sites you include; the size and complexity of each site including number of areas and employees involved; the number of permits you hold; the location of your sites; the availability of local auditors/ assessors; the maturity of your EMS; time and resource constraints; if you are seeking registration to just ISO 14001 or also to the Eco-Management Audit Scheme (EMAS) system; if you are already ISO 9001- or 9002-certified, etc. These are many of the same issues you faced when you first considered ISO 14001 implementation.

■ ISO 14000—NEW AND IMPROVED CERTIFICATION

ISO 14000 superseded the United Kingdom's BS 7750 on adoption of the ISO standard in October 1996. If your firm has already certified to the British standard through the United Kingdom Accreditation Service (UKAS—the registrar-accrediting body mandated by the British government to enforce ISO standards), upgrading to ISO 14000 is relatively simple, providing you can demonstrate that your documentation and procedures meet a total of 18 updated requirements.

UKAS director Roger Brockway was the original drafter of the pioneering British standard, years before ISO 14000 came into being. He acknowledges that the two have many similarities, but since ISO 14000 requirements are broader, previously registered companies are encouraged to be re-certified. The primary difference between the older BS 7750 and today's ISO 14000 is the acknowledgment of an environmental policy endorsing the prevention of pollution.

"There are obviously grey areas," Brockway notes. "The point of achieving accreditation is that it remains intact and that companies don't let it fritter away."

Ruth Bacon is the manager of the United Kingdom's Environmental Auditors Registration Association (EARA), which provided the Secretariat for the ISO Working Group (Technical Committee [TC]207/Sector Code [SC]2/Work Group [WG]3) that developed ISO 14012 and has, since ISO 14000's adoption, altered its registration criteria to assure compatibility with the international standard. EARA has four syllabi (Foundation Course in Environmental Auditing, Introduction to EMS Course, EMS Implementation Course, and Advanced EMS Auditing Course) against which other courses (such as those offered by Perry Johnson, Inc.) are approved, and operates a referral service for its registrants. So Bacon is in a good position to gauge the acceptance of ISO 14000, both in the United Kingdom and worldwide.

"More than 200 sites in the United Kingdom achieved certification to BS7750," she told us in late 1996, "and it is likely that they will extend this certification to ISO 14001, which can be done relatively easily—indeed, some already have. However, I believe it is a little too early to estimate the worldwide take-up of ISO 14000 by business."

Since that conversation, it has become apparent that ISO 14000 is picking up steam. Ford Motor Company has taken up the standard, announcing that it is going to certify 126 of its worldwide facilities to ISO 14001 by 1999. When a major mover-and-shaker like Ford heads in such a direction, others (principally Ford suppliers and Ford's major competition worldwide) are almost sure to follow, so it's pretty safe to say that EMS certification is here to stay.

■ WHAT'S INVOLVED IN THE ISO 14001 REGISTRATION PROCESS?

To become registered to ISO 14001, you will need the services of a fully qualified registrar. If your goal from the onset of your ISO 14001 planning stages is to seek ISO 14001 registration, it is prudent to select your registrar firm before you get into actual implementation. In this way, you will know all that is required for registration right up front, saving time, money, and resources. The sooner you contract with the ISO 14001 registrar, the better. Another reason: these companies are likely to be extremely busy in the coming months with those early birds who might be a step ahead of you. Give yourself time to evaluate your possible choices of registrar agencies. Regardless of what stage of implementation you are in when you decide to seek ISO 14001 registration, as soon as that decision has been reached, select your registrar and begin the relationship.

■ SELECTING A REGISTRAR

How do you select a registrar?

"It's a classic purchase decision," says Joseph Dunbeck of the Milwaukee-based Registrar Accreditation Board (RAB), which—in partnership with the American National Standards Institute (ANSI)—certifies registrars and individual auditors for *their* part in the ISO 14000 process. "And you should investigate the same way you'd pick any other contractor or consultant—through research, through references and by asking registrar candidates for proposals. The interview process is extremely important—you should ask for details on the registrar's experience, their knowledge—particularly within your industry—their prior registrations and the number of registrations they have performed."

The International Registrar of Certified Auditors (IRCA), another UK-based company, was one of the first accrediting bodies to offer EMS course providers (such as Perry Johnson, Inc.) the opportunity to be certified. Rod King, IRCA registrations manager, likens taking a non-certified course to taking a college course from a nonaccredited university. "Certification," he says, "is an important distinction to be acknowledged."

The RAB's Joe Dunbeck says that organizations in search of a registrar can contact his organization, but there is a caveat, "We can provide companies with a list of registrars, but we cannot recommend one over the other. There are, however, directories available which list registrars by activities and by SIC codes—these can help an organization make their initial selections."

■ READY, SET . . .

Choose your registrar early, but do not put your registrar to work until you have finished all the tasks involved in establishing an environmental management system.

Before the registrar can begin assessing your entity, your EMS must not only be in place, it must have completed the entire EMS implementation cycle. The following factors must be present:

➤ The EMS, meeting all the requirements of ISO 14001, must be documented, implemented, and in operation for a minimum of three to six months.

➤ You must have documentation outlining the organization's environmental-related procedures and commitment to prevention of pollution. EMS documentation must also meet all ISO 14001 requirements. It is a critical component of the registration assessment. That is absolutely essential to the process.

➤ Training must be provided to ensure that personnel whose job activities could potentially have a significant impact on the environment are knowledgeable about their responsibilities and are competent to perform their jobs. In addition, general EMS-awareness training must be provided to all employees; this training should include communication of the organization's environmental policy.

➤ The internal audit system must be fully operational and its effectiveness demonstrated.

➤ At least one management review must have been conducted.

These ISO 14001 registration-process guidelines were established by the European Accreditation of Certification (EAC) and are followed in the United States. A similar course is followed by the guidelines of the American accreditation alliance of ANSI and the RAB. In addition, the International Accreditation Forum (IAF) released harmonized ISO 14001 accreditation criteria early in 1997.

If your EMS meets these preliminary assessment requirements and you have established your contractual relationship with the registrar agency, then you proceed with formal ISO 14001 certification/registration (the words are used interchangeably) steps. These are:

➤ Preregistration audit (optional; see following section).

➤ Document review.

➤ Assessment of internal audit system.

➤ Registration/certification audit.

➤ Corrective action and follow-up.

➤ Issuance of registration certificate.

➤ Surveillance audits.

■ FORMAL STEPS OF THE ISO 14001 REGISTRATION PROCESS

➤ Preregistration Audit

The preregistration audit is considered optional in the United States. However, the EAC Audit Methodology includes it as part of the formal ISO 14001 registration, viewing it as a "normal function" of the process. We recommend that it be conducted as another mechanism to assist the company's ultimate goal of successfully completing the formal EMS audit.

A preregistration audit or assessment assists the auditor in understanding the company's EMS in terms of its environmental impacts and applicable regulations. It also quickly reveals the organization's state of readiness for the actual registration audit. This will be determined by reviewing the extent to which:

➤ Additional documentation has to be reviewed and/or what knowledge must be obtained in advance (including any draft environmental reports or statements).

➤ Collected information can be used to help conduct the registration audit (e.g., planning, level of expertise needed).

➤ Licenses are in place for relevant activities.

➤ The EMS is designed to meet regulatory requirements and achieve continual improvement of the organization's environmental improvement.

➤ The EMS has been implemented properly.

➤ Internal audits show that the EMS conforms with the applicable requirements of the standard and can be useful for the registration audit.

All of this information will help the registrar plan for the actual registration audit. By knowing in advance detailed information about your company's operation, the scope of your EMS, and how it appears to be addressing the ISO 14001 requirements, the registrar can determine how many auditors will be needed, what technical expertise is required, how long they will need to be on site, and other resource requirements.

During the preregistration audit, the registrar will examine the findings of your internal EMS auditing. Considerations will include:

➤ The competence, experience, training, and independence of the organization's internal auditors.

➤ The auditing procedures that have been used.

➤ What standards and references were used.

➤ How checks and verifications were performed.

➤ What resources were available for the audit(s).

➤ The audit organization.

➤ Past audit findings.

➤ Management of audit follow-up activities.

➤ Timeliness for corrective action and the effectiveness of the organization's corrective action measures.

Should the internal auditing methods, auditor qualifications, and findings prove to be in accordance with ISO 14001 standards, and also demonstrate that the EMS completely conforms with the requirements and is performing effectively, the registrar *may* reduce the scope of the formal registration audit. However, this will require verification to the accreditation body that governs registrar firm policies and procedures for EMS auditing and, frankly, it's unlikely.

During a preaudit or preassessment, the registrar is not allowed to provide any consulting to the company. The registrar may determine and evaluate the state of the company's EMS in comparison with the ISO 14001 standard. But no guidance can be provided. The result of this step may be that the company's EMS is not ready for a formal registration audit. If the preaudit is properly conducted, specific shortcomings of the EMS will surface. The registrar will document any areas of nonconformance and will report these to the organization, but ethical considerations prevent the registrar from telling its client how to correct them. There are two reasons for this: One is that information gleaned at other audited facilities cannot be passed along out of consideration for proprietary processes and confidentiality; the other is that, if the registrar provides corrective advice, it is acting as a consultant, and consultants are not permitted to audit their own clients for registration.

➤ Document Review

Some registrar agencies conduct the document review as part of the registration audit. Others complete this step beforehand. It is often referred to as a "desktop audit" and is conducted (for the sake of convenience and cost containment) at the registrar's offices, not at the site being audited. In either case, the completeness of the organization's EMS documentation can speak volumes about whether or not a formal EMS registration audit should be conducted. If all of the documentation required by ISO 14001 is not complete or is severely lacking, there is no reason to go any further in the registration process. The auditor must notify the auditee of this fact. Should the registration audit team arrive on site and find the documentation elements of ISO 14001 obviously absent, they must stop the audit. Completing a document review before the official registration audit begins will prevent this costly mishap.

This is another reason it is important to build your EMS from the perspective of the auditor. Be certain you have checked and completed all documentation requirements of ISO 14001 throughout your implementation process. Your internal auditors should also pay close attention to this in their internal auditing. Documentation is the backbone of the ISO 14001 EMS.

➤ Registration Audit

The same steps that you applied during your internal audits will occur during the formal registration audit. It will start with an opening meeting that will cover the scope and nature of the audit. There should be daily briefings to discuss any needed adjustments to schedules, as well as running updates on what the auditors have seen.

The team of auditors will work their way through your site assessing how your EMS has been integrated throughout each area that could have a significant environmental impact. Auditors will be interviewing employees. The ead auditor will ask for controlled copies of your EMS documentation.

Key documentation includes:

➤ Your environmental policy.

➤ Your EMS manual (if you have one), EMS procedures, and work instructions.

➤ Environmental assessments identifying your major environmental aspects and significant impacts of your organization's products, activities, and services.

➤ A list of applicable legal and other requirements to which your organization subscribes.

➤ Objectives and targets for your significant environmental impacts.

➤ Environmental management program(s) description(s) identifying your approach for meeting your defined objectives and targets.

This documentation will be reviewed to ensure consistency between your environmental policy, objectives, targets, and programs. Documentation will be evaluated to see that it is consistent with, and designed to reduce, the environmental impacts identified in your environmental assessments. The registrar's auditors will look for evidence that you are tracking the progress of your environmental management programs and that you are periodically reporting to top management on your organization's progress or opportunities for improvement.

Auditors will look for objective evidence that your organization has defined goals, responsibility, and authority for implementation and maintenance of the EMS and associated environmental programs. Your management representative(s) should be readily identifiable, and their roles and authority to develop, implement, and maintain the EMS should be clearly spelled out in your EMS documentation. Responsibility for, and resources needed to, implement the environmental management program(s) must be clearly defined. All requirements from ISO 14001 Section 4.4.1 (Structure and Responsibility) must be met. The verbiage should be such that a stranger to the system should be able to read the documentation and understand it.

Additional documentation for audit review will include training records for all employees—especially those working on products or activities associated with significant environmental aspects. A training-needs analysis must be available for your organization, identifying the training required for each employee. A matrix, showing employment positions on one side and available training courses across the top, is a common format used to depict the training-needs analysis.

All employees must have had the EMS policy communicated to them. They should be aware of the importance of conformance with the policy and EMS procedures. Personnel working in areas with significant environmental aspects must have additional training. In addition to being qualified on the basis of education and/or experience, they need to be aware of the significant environmental impacts, actual or potential, of their work, and the environmental benefits to be gained through improved personal performance. They also need to know the potential consequences of departure from standard operating procedures.

All employees need to know their roles and responsibilities in achieving conformance with the environmental policy and procedures, and with the requirements of the EMS—including emergency preparedness and response requirements.

Records of internal and external communications with interested parties (employee suggestions, complaints from neighbors or concerned citizens, inquiries from regulatory agencies, etc.) and related procedures will be looked at to determine if the interests of these parties have played a role in determining your significant environmental impacts and associated objectives and targets. How you receive, document, and respond to these interests, and how you record your decisions with respect to their concerns, must be documented in procedure(s) and environmental records of correspondence and decision making.

The auditors will look at your organization's operational controls and procedures, and at operating criteria for any activities, products, or services associated with potential or actual identified significant environmental aspects and impacts. If these activities are controlled with work instructions, the auditors may ask your operators to explain, identify, or demonstrate these.

Emergency preparedness will also be evaluated during the audit. Emergency plans, procedures, and facilities, and the results of past emergency drills will be some of the things for which auditors will look. If you've had any environmental accidents, auditors will probably ask to see any records of the follow-up investigations, and of changes made to the emergency preparedness program as a result.

Monitoring of key elements associated with significant environmental impacts is another area auditors will investigate. Procedures for the operation and maintenance of environmentally related monitoring equipment will be reviewed. Calibration records for this equipment must be available. Measurement capabilities and units will be compared with any performance indicators tied to objectives and targets established for the activity or activities being monitored.

The ISO 14001 EMS audit is *not* a compliance audit; it does not specifically investigate to see if all laws and regulations are being met, nor is it necessarily accepted as proof of obedience to pertinent environmental laws and regulations. That caveat aside, the audit *will* require documentation and demonstration of the procedure(s) used to ensure compliance with such regulations.

You'll also need to provide results of internal audits, corrective and preventive actions taken to eliminate nonconformances, and records of management review meetings. The auditors will evaluate the qualifications of your internal auditors (training and experience), the soundness of your audit program and procedures, and the preventive-action efforts. Management review meetings must include evaluations, by top management, of the continuing suitability, adequacy, and effectiveness of the EMS. The need for changes to policy, or other elements of the EMS, must also have been evaluated. The documentation must clearly communicate to the auditor that all of these elements were discussed; use of an agenda or checklist with meeting notes is the best way to meet this requirement.

How well you control the documentation of the EMS, including how you identify, maintain, and dispose of your environmental records, will also be examined. A document control system—identical, or virtually identical, to that used in an ISO 9000 system—is required. This should be fully conformant to the requirements of ISO 14001 Sections 4.4.5 (Document Control) and 4.5.3 (Records).

As mentioned earlier, you'll get running daily evaluations from the audit team subsequent to each day of the audit. Nonconformities may be discovered along the way; if so, this is not the end of the world. It's still possible to obtain certification; it will just take longer.

Nonconformities will be conveyed to you in "Nonconformance Reports" (NCRs), a standard form that records the exact nature and location of an individual nonconformity, and the specific part of ISO 14001 that applies. You must acknowledge your awareness of the nonconformity by signing the report. In this way, you'll be well aware of your standing before the final meeting with the audit team.

At the closing meeting, you'll learn the audit team's recommendation to the registrar with regard to certification. If the audit went well, the lead auditor may recommend "immediate certification"—which means you'll get a copy of the report within a fortnight, and a certificate in four to six weeks.

➤ Corrective Action and Follow-Up

Minor nonconformities will require you to provide proof of corrective measures to the registrar; these measures must include internal-auditor follow-up to verify that the measures were effective. The registrar's lead auditor may elect to revisit the site to personally observe the correction. Once corrective actions have been verified by the registrar, the nonconformities are "closed out," and certification may proceed.

Major nonconformities—indications that major parts of the EMS are missing or dysfunctional, and significant detrimental impacts are possible—will sometimes require another *full* audit before certification is considered. The auditor will apprise you of your options before concluding the final meeting.

■ CHECK, PLEASE . . .

How much all of this costs depends on how well you've planned your purchase of registrar services, how efficiently you've facilitated it (e.g., if the desktop audit has to be performed at your facility, it is more costly than simply sending the documentation to the registrar), what follow-up is necessary, and how complex your organization is. Simplicity and doing things right the first time will pay dividends in the form of lower audit costs.

Marketing Your Environmental Position

Truth will rise above falsehood as oil above water.

—MIGUEL DE CERVANTES

C ertification will require time and effort, so when you do all the right things to gain ISO 14000 certification you ought to be able to display your status in ways that increase sales, reassure investors, and convince the public that your company's environmental vision will ultimately serve them best.

While you can reap the many benefits of marketing your environmentally friendly image, this is one area of image-building in which you want to proceed with great care and caution. The public has grown cynical about the environmental claims of businesses. For a generation now, too many organizations have worked under the false assumption that it is easier to change an image than to change a reality. Hundreds of billions have been spent hiring Washington lobbyists to improve environmental images.

Most of this image-building, however, amounted to little more than "whitewashing," or in the environmental vernacular, "greenwashing." You have only to walk through any supermarket to find labels declaring greenness from every shelf; yet the only thing green about many of these products is the color of oil-based printer's ink on the package. Ambiguous wording—"Earth Friendly," "Nature's," "Nonpolluting," or just big letters spelling, "GREEN"—is everywhere. As a result, businesses themselves have fostered a credibility gap, and even honest expressions of environmental integrity are often met with skepticism.

The framers of ISO 14000 anticipated the difficulty of advertising certification, and of creating genuine credibility for the standards and standard-certified companies. The ISO 14020 labeling standards will be reviewed later in this chapter. But before dealing with these specifics, it is essential to examine the prospect of marketing your company's ISO 14000 environmental image, the pitfalls, and the proven benefits.

There has never been an era before in which the subject of marketing was more important. Because of electronic communication, we live in a global village, where international business and consumer markets are expanding everywhere. Today, no walls can impede the free flow of information.

Consider what that means to business. William Odom, Chairman of Ford Credit, the largest automotive financing institution in the world, put it this way, "Word-of-mouth advertising has always had the greatest impact on our reputations, and on our ability to grain new customers and retain old ones. Today, the back fence is the computer keyboard. When someone gossips about you on the Internet, the entire world hears it instantaneously. That's anything but small talk."

This unprecedented publicity works in favor of companies that are thoroughly committed to environmental management. 3M Corporation is perhaps the grandfather example of that kind of highly visible commitment. 3M made its environmental stance public in 1975, when the company began its efforts, appropriately enough, with its own employees. 3M announced its "3P" program, which stood for "Pollution Prevention Pays." It was an environmentally focused suggestion program that rewarded employees with both money and recognition for coming up with ways to reduce emissions and eliminate process waste.

Since its inception, that one effort has produced savings that now approach a billion dollars, but, even more importantly, it has fostered an environmental culture over the years.

Numerous environmental efforts, and research programs, have given 3M an earned public reputation as one of America's most committed environmental leaders. And 3M continues to demonstrate that integrity in many ways.

One government innovation in recent years has been to sell pollution permits, with the income presumably going to general pollution-control efforts. If a company does not use its pollution allowance, it can sell its permits to another company, thus creating a financial incentive to meet and surpass regulatory standards. 3M made environmental news a few years ago when it announced that its unused pollution permits would not be sold, but given back to the government. As a 3M spokesperson said, "In this way, when we make an environmental improvement, it will be an environmental improvement."

The 3M Company has received dozens of awards over the years from local, state, and federal agencies and environmental groups for its leadership. It was named as one of the first companies to participate in the Environmental Protection Agency's "Excellence in Leadership" program, which gives a company a blanket environmental permit, so the company is not burdened in meeting separate, and potentially conflicting, detailed regulations.

Yet 3M has accomplished all of this with only modest investments over the years in environmental advertising, following a philosophy that actions are the best advertisement of all.

If your environmental effort is complete and company-wide, then your efforts will receive a great deal of interest, and unpaid editorial coverage, all by themselves. As Robert P. Bringer, 3M's vice president of environmental engineering, says, "When business interests are merged with environmental interests, good things happen."

The benefits, Bringer suggests, show up in lower costs, higher quality, fewer liabilities, employee morale, and "an enhanced corporate reputation that results in more marketable products."

Many other companies prove the benefit of marketing their environmental management. Companies like Aubrey Organics, Calvert Group, Levi Strauss, Real Goods, Monsanto, Target Stores, Viacom, Ben & Jerry's, and The Body Shop, largely agree that in crowded markets, environmental advertising delineates them from the competition. This is especially significant in markets with inherently generic products, where there is little apparent difference in one box of soap or one bank and another. Their image gives these companies a competitive edge, and is particularly valuable when the economy is down, and product sales are slow.

Co-op America's National Green Pages lists 1,800 businesses, from manufactured products to clothing, foods, insurance, banks, and a telephone company called Working Assets Long Distance. Studies show that at least 65 percent of all Americans say they will reject one product, and purchase another, on the basis of its environmental image. Actual purchases suggest the number is smaller, but even if it is only 25 percent, that is a significant market segment. And for hard-core environmentalists, who subscribe and live by publications like Co-op America's National Green Page companies, this vocal minority is so thoroughly committed as to actually *keep* hundreds of companies in business.

Yet it is not necessary to amass decades of environmental management success, like 3M or Ben & Jerry's, to successfully market a positive image. The public seems to love repentant sinners. Companies with poor reputations can often turn their image around overnight by making a visible and believable commitment.

McDonald's achieved such a conversion. McDonald's staunchly continued to use and defend polystyrene packaging throughout the 1980s, even under visible public attacks, including a widely publicized boycott of McDonald's by schoolchildren, the company's core consumer group. Finally in 1990, McDonald's switched to paper wrappers, and heavily publicized it as an environmental decision. That same year, McDonald's announced a new alliance with the highly respected Environmental Defense Fund. McDonald's contracted the Fund to examine the company's 11,000 restaurants to find ways to reduce solid wastes and reuse materials, and to improve the environment. McDonald's stock and sales went up. More importantly, McDonald's continues with its environmental management efforts, and, like 3M, is beginning to build lasting public trust.

Once you've made significant environmental efforts, you may and should advertise them. But be aware that, when it comes to indicating your sincerity, media coverage is your best means of communication. Seeing a claim in an ad is one thing, but seeing the same thing in a newspaper report or magazine article, or hearing about it on a radio or TV news program, is another.

So put your public relations people to work on the subject, as well as your ad agency. Ethics still apply, and the media will not accept as newsworthy anything that is not truly news, but when you've made progress, announce it in the fourth estate. It's your surest method of building credibility.

Recognized credibility is the goal of environmental marketing efforts. That is why the ISO 14000 designers have taken such pains to develop a system that can live up to third-party audits, and can achieve third-party accreditation under ISO 14001. In keeping with the goal of company flexibility, ISO has not chosen to mandate how, and in what form, a company can promote ISO 14001 certification, with one notable exception—labeling. ISO 14020 is an Environmental Labeling standard that, in the words of the standard, "provides general guidance to help organizations develop specific environmental claims. ISO 14020 streamlines the Federal Trade Commission's guidelines and can be used as a tool by purchasers for selecting products and services."

There are three label types under ISO 14020. These cover 14001 certified company products; self-declared claims; and specific product information that has been independently verified. Yet no matter what the type of label, the same overriding rule applies: Claims *must* be substantiated. Every environmental claim has to be followed with a clear statement such as, "This information has been verified by ABC Auditors" or "Based on inspection and verification from the Environmental Protection Agency."

To maintain that level of credibility, the ISO technical committees have devised a set of advertising label standards that can assist your company in establishing a credible public image. Vague terms (e.g., "new and improved," "recycled," "earth friendly") are simply not permitted. If you are going to say it, substantiate it.

In addition to 14020 Basic Principles, a series of standards address labeling. They include:

ISO 14021 Labeling—Terms and Definitions provides definitions for the labeling terminologies and technologies in use.

ISO 14022 Labeling—Self-Declaration of Environmental Claims closely follows the Federal Trade Commission in defining the principles for using environmental symbols.

ISO 14023 Labeling—Self-Declared Claims, Testing and Verification Methodology establishes the principles for substantiating claims through scientifically sound testing and verification that must be reproducible and repeatable.

ISO 14024 Labeling—Guiding Principles for Multiple Criteria-Based Practitioner Programs (Type One Programs) establishes standards for broad-based environmental certification efforts like Green Seal or Blue Angel. With this standard, ISO practitioners can substantiate and evaluate product claims and award special recognition labels to companies.

The purpose of the entire ISO 14020 series is to raise the standards of environmental claims. The intent is to make labeling, and by suggestion advertising in general, more credible and responsible. It stresses minimizing unwarranted claims and providing accurate verification for every claim made.

An obvious benefit in this approach is that it reduces confusion and eco-marketing obfuscation for consumers, who can thus make more informed choices about products that make legitimate environmental claims. Raising the public confidence level in environmental advertising will also benefit the environment, by encouraging companies to improve their products, processes, and services in ways that are both verifiable, and marketable.

Yet ISO 14020 series offers only minimal direction on how to market your environmental efforts. It stresses what to print on your labels, not the soul-searching process you'll need to follow in deciding what marketing theme or approach can best serve your unique industry and product lines. As with all business strategies, your approach to promoting your environmental image should be distinctly your own.

The best way to develop an image strategy, however, is to first find out just what your customers and publics actually think of your current efforts. Most major corporations today take the public pulse regularly with customer-satisfaction surveys. If your company has such a structure, and it is dynamic (i.e., you contact the customers, rather than waiting for them to call you or send in a registration form), it is relatively easy to incorporate a few environmental questions in the mix. These efforts are essential to determine public perception of your company's credibility regarding environmental stewardship.

Perception is not always reality. But it is fundamental to know what the perception is before you design an effort that will communicate your actual commitment.

Begin by assuming a knowledgeable audience. Too often, environmental advertisers either state the obvious or obviously overstate the importance of their point.

A major automobile company, for example, has presented a series of ads over the past decade praising itself for environmental and safety achievements that are required by law, and that every other auto company must have to legally sell its products. Such environmental marketing only serves as an embarrassment to the company. Another company, a major airline, in fact, ran ads after Earth Day a few years ago, praising itself for recycling beverage cans while ignoring the high petroleum consumption and pollution produced by jet fuels. When you trivialize the issues, you trivialize your efforts.

If you are going to market your environmental image, remember that you are attempting to develop a public perception, and such image-building takes time. Infrequent or one-time environmental advertising efforts and publicity campaigns rarely change attitudes. Make your image a part of your ongoing corporate identity effort, and a long-term merchandising goal.

In the information age, whatever environmental claims you make will be scrutinized thoroughly by government agencies, by environmental watchdog groups, and perhaps even more diligently by informed and sophisticated electronics-age consumers.

ISO 14001 certification, and other environmental management programs, cannot act as a green carpet under which you may sweep the dust of your company's ecological past. There is simply too high a probability of exposure, and too large a price to pay from backlash. So if any portion of your operations is not sincerely working at improvement, if any division or department will not stand scrutiny, it is best not to advertise environmental awareness at all.

Yet with ISO 14000, your organization should not need to worry about flagrant violations of public sensibilities. ISO 14001 is a companywide system that enlists every person

in your organization, and audits every environmental outcome, always with an eye to continual improvement. So
even when shortcomings are exposed, they are made in an
atmosphere of openness, and always with articulated plans
on how your company plans to improve the situation. There
can even be something noble about failures in such a context because they represent genuine effort.

It is in trying, in the clear commitment to improving
your environment, that you will establish your credibility as
a company that cares about the community, the planet, and
the future.

Postscript

The Business of Being Human

Never before has man had such capacity to control his environment . . . We have the power to make this the best generation of mankind in the history of the world—or to make it the last.

—JOHN F. KENNEDY

B usiness is inherently pragmatic. We are more concerned about how many pins can dance off the end of an assembly line per hour than the theological question of how many angels can dance on the head of a pin. This book, therefore, has provided a presentation of ISO 14000 that emphasizes its immediate and practical benefits.

The decision to incorporate ISO 14001 into your organization can be justified entirely on pragmatic considerations. To recount just a few of the numerous benefits, they include:

➤ Cost reductions in operating and materials savings through systemic management.

➤ Global opportunities by living up to standards expected, or soon required, by customers and suppliers in other markets.

➤ Process controls that reduce paperwork and training costs through a structured approach, thus increasing productivity.

➤ Greater access to financial capital, lower insurance rates, and higher shareholder confidence by reassuring the financial community that you are managing environmental risks.

➤ High probability of being treated with greater deference and cooperation by government regulators looking to shift from costly command and control to free market leadership; associated savings in avoiding fines and even criminal penalties.

➤ Savings through integration of environmental management with quality, health, and safety management as ISO 14000 blends with ISO 9000, TQM, and other improvement cycle based systems.

➤ A continual improvement system in place, that allows an organization to demonstrate improvement and to anticipate future environmental demands.

➤ A certifiable image of environmental awareness, resulting in motivated employees, a marketable public image, and measurable sales opportunities.

The list of tangible, and implied, benefits could go on for pages without ever mentioning the fundamental reason for environmental management—to reduce pollution and conserve resources, and to improve the quality of air, water, and land, and the quality of life, for ourselves and for generations yet unborn.

We avoid these terms in justifying ISO 14001 because they sound a little too soft for pragmatic businesspeople; too nebulous to be measured and reported out in quarterly returns or at stockholder meetings. Yet this vague issue of achieving a sustainable environment may be more of a defining factor in your company's future than all of the measurable bottom-line considerations combined.

■ ENVIRONMENTAL FAILURE

Why? Because this is only the beginning of the environmental age. The environmental challenges are increasing exponentially, and our best efforts to turn the trend around have had as much impact as a water pick on the Towering Inferno. Paul Hawken, environmentalist and author, said it best: "If every company on the planet were to adopt the best environmental practices of the 'leading' companies . . . the world would still be moving toward sure degradation and collapse." Earth's environment is degrading, and our resources are depleting, and, by all measures, will continue get worse well into the 21st century.

Three major factors complicate the challenge—world population, industrial growth, and advanced technologies.

➤ Population Growth

World population will grow to 10 *billion* people by 2030, which to put into perspective, is more than three times as many people that existed on this planet in the 1950s.

Dramatic efforts to curb population growth, especially in China and other Asian states, have slowed the rate of growth, but because of an ever-larger population base, the absolute population numbers will continue skyward for the foreseeable future. About 95 percent of these new people will be in what are now considered Third World, or under-developed, countries.

Population increases of this magnitude do not equate to market opportunities in much of the Third World, simply because so many of these nations have already used up their environmental capital. A number of countries—about 40 percent of the world's current population—already are limited in their ability to farm their lands because of a lack of water. Constant agriculture has leached the earth of its nutrients, and leaves the land barren. All natural resources are being consumed far faster than they can be replaced, and some are simply not replaceable at all. Every year humans consume fossil fuels that took a million years to develop. World Bank places more than half of the world's populations in a position of "near environmental bankruptcy."

With ever more limited salable resources, Third World countries are running up immense foreign debts, which with even greater population growth, suggests an improbability of these debts ever being addressed or retired. Third World debt is now the largest problem facing global economic growth, especially in Africa, South America, and segments of Asia. The result may be literal, as well as environmental, bankruptcy.

➤ Industrial Growth

Industrialization is the second challenge. The global economy has nearly quintupled in size since the 1950s. Rising industrialization raises the standard of living, improves the quality of life, and increases longevity, wherever it develops. And with globalization, the Third World nations, especially in the areas of the Pacific Rim and India, are experiencing unprecedented industrial growth. Five times the growth rate, in fact, of the established industrial West.

Yet each of these success stories amounts to a net loss to the planet. For a single individual in a wealthy industrial nation consumes far more energy and resources, placing a far greater proportional burden on the ecosystem. Today, less than 20 percent of the world's population, in the developed nations, consume about 75 percent of the earth's energy and resources. Individual mobility—by car, train, and planes—is by far the greatest consumer of energy. What will happen when global industrialization is successful and the other 80 percent of this planet's inhabitants are able to consume five times as much as they did as Third World peoples?

In every aspect of life, living better now translates to consuming more and leads to the paradox of our age. It can best be characterized by the story of King Pyrrhus of Epirus, who fought and won a series of battles against the Romans, yet suffered tremendous losses with every success. Finally, King Pyrrhus cried out: "One more victory and all will be lost." Each victory in industrial globalization, in raising the standard of life for humankind, may be purchased at an ever increasing cost, until we experience a pyrrhic victory, in which additional success could mean environmental collapse. To look at it another way, Thomas Malthus assumed the limit was food production, yet today many are asking if the limit is success itself.

➤ The Price of Growth Technology

The third concern is advanced technologies. There is virtually no question that the assumption today is that technology can be the ultimate panacea, the elixir that will cure all these environmental challenges. There is no question that it is powerful medicine. The miraculous advances made in electronics technology, both in knowledge applications and hardware design, in the past two decades is the primary reason that we have been able to reduce pollution levels, both mobile and stationary, and are finding ever more innovative ways to modify and recycle materials. The most advanced technologies are the cleanest, least costly technologies.

Yet even this scenario has inherent difficulties. First, is that advanced technologies require fewer and fewer people for production at the very time when there are more and more people in need of work. This creates its own paradox in heavily populated nations moving toward industrialization, for the more they use advanced technologies to leap over the undesirable aspects of environmental degradation and achieve efficient modern industries, the greater their unemployment becomes. Thus in many rapidly industrializing Asian nations, unemployment is rising even faster than gross national product.

Another challenge to technological solutions is that they are costly. In many markets, the public may be unwilling, or unable, to bear the full cost of these technologies of environmentally superior products. With environmental management systems like ISO 14000, initial costs of controls are more than offset by savings in materials and in increased efficiencies. This is true for the first 75 to 85 percent of most environmental efforts. Yet it is like ladling water from a barrel. The first efforts are easy, and produce a full ladle every time, but as businesses get down to the bottom of the barrel on improvements, each dip of the ladle brings up less, so costs more. Often, at this point, the answer is to get a new barrel, to shift to entirely new alternative technologies. A shift from gasoline to electric powered vehicles, for example. Yet these new technologies require tremendous expense in going through the learning curve, and in establishing new infrastructures. And the question becomes—when do advanced technologies for environmental improvements outstrip consumers' ability to pay for them?

Also, while market-driven solutions work best, they can only work when the actual value of energy and materials depletion and scarcity is reflected in its price and availability. The United States is a prime example of a country whose government's policies actually have a negative impact on the environment and make market-driven solutions all but impossible. The United States is one of the few nations that still keeps the price of oil artificially low, and thus continues to have difficulty motivating its people to purchase fuel-efficient cars and trucks. In California, the U.S. government sells water that ought to cost as much as $350 per thousand cubic meters in that environment, for less than three dollars. And every summer, government pleads with the public to conserve water while removing all economic incentive to do so.

The United States is not the only offender. Many, if not most, nations underwrite their own home energy and materials industries rather than shifting their support from these existing infrastructures to alternative renewable resources or advanced technologies. And because there is no global uniformity, energy and environmental taxes—when they are employed—can actually penalize home industries in competition against unregulated global competitors.

All businesspeople need to understand that we have not turned the environmental tide and that far higher environmental seas are on the horizon. With population and industrial growth both rising, we are only at the beginning of an era where environmental concern becomes an ever-increasing aspect of our existence, and an ever more significant cost of doing business.

So while ISO 14001 has immediate practical value, its greater value may well be that it can put into place a system not only for responding to current ecological concerns, but for anticipating and preparing to respond to the dramatic environmental changes that lie ahead.

ISO 14001 provides an infrastructure for cooperation among business, government, environmentalists, and the public, that while beneficial today, may be critical in addressing larger environmental challenges tomorrow.

Science-fiction writer Ray Bradbury once was asked if he thought his book *Fahrenheit 451* was an accurate prediction of the future. Bradbury replied, "Good Lord, no! I'm not trying to predict the future. All I want to do is to prevent it."

In addressing these challenges now, we may well be able to prevent the worst-case scenarios in our environmental future. And ISO 140001 can be the first realistic step in the direction of a sustainable global environment and genuine stewardship of the Earth.

Bibliography

An Environmental Agenda for the Future. Coveto, CA: Island Press, 1989.

Bailey, Ronald (Ed.). *The True State of the Planet.* New York: Simon & Schuster, 1995.

Brown, Lester. *State of the World: 1996.* Worldwatch Institute. New York: W. W. Norton, 1996.

Brown, Lester. *Vital Signs: 1996.* Worldwatch Institute. New York: W. W. Norton, 1996.

Budiansky, Stephen. *Nature's Keepers—The New Science of Nature Management.* New York: Free Press, 1995.

Carson, Rachel. *Silent Spring.* Boston: Houghton Mifflin, 1973.

Carson, Patrick, and Moulden, Julia. *Green Is Gold.* New York: Harper Collins, 1996.

Cascio, Joseph (Ed.). *ISO 14000 Guide.* New York: McGraw-Hill, 1996.

Cascio, Joseph (Ed.). *ISO 14000 Handbook.* Fairfax, VA: CEEM Information Services, 1996.

Clements, Richard. *Complete Guide to ISO 14000.* Englewood Cliffs, NJ: Prentice Hall, 1996.

Coleman, David. *Ecopolitics.* Chapel Hill, NC: Green Movement, 1996.

Duchin, Faye, and Lange, Glenn-Mario. *The Future of the Environment*. Oxford, UK: Oxford University Press, 1994.

Gore, Albert. *Earth in the Balance*. New York: Penguin Books, 1994.

Grover, Ralph. Personal Interview. December 18, 1996.

Hawken, Paul. *The Ecology of Commerce*. New York: Harper Business, 1993.

Hemenway, Caroline G. *What Is ISO 14000? Questions & Answers*. Fairfax, VA: CEEM Information Services, 1995.

Jain, Urban, and Stacey, Balback. *Environmental Assessment*. New York: McGraw-Hill, 1993.

Johnson, Scott David. *An Analysis of the Relationship Between Corporate Environmental and Economic*. Ann Arbor, MI: UMI Dissertation Services, 1995.

Klassen, Robert David. *The Implications of Environmental Management*. Ann Arbor, MI: UMI Dissertation Services, 1995.

Koretzky, Joseph. Written Questionnaire. June 20, 1996.

Lang, Brenda. Telephone Conversation. July 18, 1996.

Leaky, Richard. *The Sixth Extinction*. New York: Anchor Books, 1995.

Makower, Joel. *The E Factor*. New York: Tilden Press Inc., 1993.

Makower, Joel. *The Green Consumer*. New York: Penguin Books., 1993.

Managing Planet Earth. New York: Scientific American, Environmental Series, 1996.

Pacific Reserve Institute. *Free Market Environmentalism*. Oxford, UK: Oxford University Press, 1988.

Rockefeller, Nelson. *Our Environment Can Be Saved*. New York: Doubleday, 1978.

Ross, Marc, and Williams, Robert. *Our Energy: Regaining Control*. New York: McGraw-Hill, 1981.

Sandler, Blair Witten. *Enterprise, Value, Environment*. Ann Arbor, MI: UMI Dissertation Services, 1995.

Sayre, Don. *Inside ISO 14000*. Delray Beach, FL: St. Lucie Press, 1996.

Seipke, Denise Wecker. Personal Interview. December 18, 1996.

Sessions, George (Ed.). *Deep Ecology for the 21st Century*. Boston: Shambhahja, 1995.

The ISO 14000 Resource Directory. Fairfax, VA: CEEM Information Services, 1996.

Vogt, Gordon, and Wargo, Vogt. *Ecosystems*. New York: Springer-Verlag, 1996.

Wen, Chao-tung. *Integrating Environmental Management into Product*. Ann Arbor, MI: UMI Dissertation Services, 1994.

Index

A

Accountability, 80, 93
Adam, Ansel, 17
Advertising, 213–214
Air, environmental concerns, 177–178
Allaire, Paul, 13
All-inclusive procedures, 136
American Express, 12
American National Standards Institute (ANSI), 193, 195
Andean Pack, 36
Arm & Hammer, 16
AT&T, 16
Attitude, change in, 9–10
Aubrey Organics, 212
Audit, environmental, generally:
    defined, 66
    documentation and, 100
    periodic, 122
    personnel involved in, generally, 93
    preregistration, 196–199
    purpose of, 113
Auditors:
    registration process, 199–204
    function of, generally, 59
Audit team, defined, 66
Automotive industry, 11, 14, 19–20, 32, 73

B

Backup files, recordkeeping guidelines, 140
Bacon, Ruth, 192
Bath & Body Works, 16
Belorussia, 36
Ben & Jerry's, 16, 212–213

Best management practices, 10

Bhopal Chemical, 4

Biohazards, 178

Bissonette, George, 22

Body Shop, The, 212

Bottom-line profitability, 12–13

Bringer, Robert P., 212

Bristol Myers, 8

British Standards Institution, 40

Brockway, Roger, 191–192

BS 5750, 45

BS 7750, 40–41, 45–46, 191–192

Burial money, 35

Business Ethics, 16

C

Calvert Group, 16, 212

Canon, Inc., 9, 19

Carson, Rachel, 30

Central American Common Market, 36

CEO (Chief Executive Officer), function of, 80, 85, 151

Certification, ISO 14000, 191–193

Changes, impact of, 154–156, 159

Chaos theory, 111–112

Chatburn, Graham, 11

Chemical Ricoh, 19

Chernobyl, 4

Chlorofluorocarbons (CFCs), 20, 25

Clean Air Act, 32

Clinton, Bill, 42

Closed out conformities, 204

Closing meeting, registration process, 204

Command and control strategy:

global, 36–38

impact of, 9, 222

overview, 33–36

Commitment:

by leadership, 25

Section 4 requirements (ISO 14001), 84

significance of, 115–117, 164, 166

Communication:

of environmental policy, 82

procedures for, 121

in registration process, 201–202

Section 4 requirements (ISO 14001), 96–98

Computer files, recordkeeping guidelines, 140

Conformance, benefits of, 3–5

Continual improvement:
  impact of, 162, 218, 222
  procedures and, 144–145,
    156
  Section 4 requirements
    (ISO 14001), 61–63,
    83–84
Continuous improvement,
  62
Contractors, 94
Co-op America, 16
  National Green Pages,
    213
Coordinator, environmental,
  function of, 21, 93
Corporate Environmental
  Data Clearinghouse
  (CEDC), 17
Corrective actions:
  procedures and, 154
  registration process, 196,
    199, 203–204
  Section 4 requirements
    (ISO 14001),
    102–104
Cradle-to-grave concepts,
  113, 122, 130
Credibility, environmental
  marketing, 214–215
Credibility gap, 210
Credit rating companies,
  15
Customer satisfaction surveys,
  216

D

Declarations, environmental,
  114
Delaney, Wilma, 9
Department of Justice, 10
Desktop audit, 199, 205
Documentation, in
  environmental
  management system:
control of, 98–100,
    139–140, 203–204
preregistration process, 197
registration process, 195,
    200–201
review of, 199
Section 4 requirements
    (ISO 14001), 85–86,
    98–100
types of, overview, 51–53,
    113–114
Dow Chemical, 34–35
Drucker, Peter, 25
Dunbeck, Joe, 194

E

Earth Summit, 38–41
East Germany, 35
EcoDeposit accounts, 16
Eco-Management and Audit
  Scheme (EMAS), 8,
  40–41

Ecosystem, interrelationship
    in, 111
Eicher, Lawrence, 39
Emergency conditions, 88
Emergency preparedness
    program, 101–102, 202
Empowerment, of employees,
    20–23, 49, 145, 153
EN 14001, 8
Environment, defined, 63–64
Environmental aspect:
    defined, 64
    types of, 87–89
Environmental assessment,
    200–201
Environmental Auditors
    Registration Association
    (EARA), 192
Environmental awareness,
    impact of, 130, 145, 153
Environmental Bankers
    Association, 15
Environmental Defense Fund,
    213
Environmental degradation,
    35, 42
Environmental impact:
    air concerns, 177–178
    defined, 64–65
    generally, 180–181
    implementation and,
        127–130
    land concerns, 179–180
    water concerns, 178–179

Environmental Management
    Procedures, 52
Environmental management
    programs, 91–92,
    147–153
Environmental management
    system (EMS), generally:
    audit, defined, 66, 106–107
    defined, (ISO/DIS 14001),
        65–66
    documentation, 98–100
    function of, 5–6
    pyramid, 115
Environmental performance
    indicators (EPIs),
    146–147
Environmental policy
    statements, 51–52. *See
    also* Policy,
    environmental
Environmental Protection
    Agency:
    development of, 34
    "Excellence in Leadership"
        program, 212
    Project XL (eXcellence in
        Leadership), 10
Environmental review, 151
Environmental Self
    Assessment Program,
    37
Equipment, operation and
    maintenance of, 202
Ethics, 150, 214

European Accreditation of
Certification (EAC),
195–196
European Economic
Community, 36
European Union, 8, 40, 190
External communication,
97–98
Exxon *Valdez*, 4, 37

F

Failure, environmental
factors:
advanced technologies,
225–228
industrial growth, 224–225
population growth,
223–224
procedures and, 153
Federal Express, 16
Federal Register, 33
Federal Trade Commission,
214
Fire safety, 93–94
Flexibility, significance of, 7,
9–10, 23, 214
Fluke Corporation, 21–22
Follow-through, 165
Follow-up, registration
process, 204–205
Ford Motor Company, 8, 11,
124, 192–193

Fuji Electric Company Ltd., 8
Fujitsu, 19
Fuller, Buckminster, 31

G

Gap analysis, 129
General Agreement on Tariffs
and Trade (GATT), 37
Germany, 8, 14, 33
Global Environmental
Management Initiatives
(GEMI), 37
Global Metallurgical, 23–24
Government intervention,
31–32, 112
Government regulation:
historical perspective,
34–35
impact of, 34–35, 118,
129–130
Great Britain, 8, 33, 40
Great Lakes Box Corporation,
124
Green Business Letter, The,
13
Green Money Journal, 16
Greenpeace, 24
Green political parties, 33
Greenwashing, 17, 210
Gro Harle Brundtland, 38
Group meeting, 85
Grover, Ralph, 163, 176

H

Hallmark, 16
Hart, Stuart, 13
Hawken, Paul, 223
Historical perspective:
  command and control
    strategy, 33–36
  European countries,
    32–33
  global command and
    control, 36–38
  government intervention,
    31–34
  International Organization
    for Standardization
    (I.S.O.), 38–42
  the 1960's, 31–32
Hitachi, 8
Holistic approach, to
  environment, 112–113
Home Depot, 16
Honeywell, 16

I

Image development, 18–20,
  210, 216–217
Immediate certification, 204
Implementation:
  building process, 117–122
  chaos theory and, 111–113
  commitment and, 115–117
  cycle, 78
  documentation, 113–115
  environmental impacts,
    127–130
  environmental policy,
    122–127
  procedures and, 131
Incentive programs, 150–151
Industrialization, impact of,
  224–225
Integration, 162–168
Intel, 10
Interested party, defined,
  69–71
Internal audit:
  auditors, *see* Internal
    auditors
  benefits of, 172
  internal team, 172–173
  interview tips, 183–184
  nonconformities, 184
  registration process and,
    203
  registration requirements,
    195
Internal auditors:
  advice for, 183–184
  in preregistration process,
    197
  selection of, 173–175
  training for, 176–182
  value of, 184–185
International Accreditation
  Forum (IAF), 195

International Chamber of
    Commerce, "Business
    Charter for Sustainable
    Development," 37
International Electrochemical
    Commission (IEC), 39
International Organization for
    Standardization (I.S.O.),
    7, 38–42
International Registrar of
    Certified Auditors
    (IRCA), 194
Investors, environmental
    management system and,
    14–16
ISO Environmental
    Management System
    Technical Committee, 24
ISO 9000, compared with ISO
    14000/14001, 6–7, 23,
    39, 45, 48–50, 70, 127,
    168, 204, 222
ISO 9001, 127
ISO 9002, 168
ISO 9660, 7
ISO 11200 Series, 39
ISO 14000, generally:
    defined, 6
    design of, 7
    disclosure laws and,
        17–18
    employee empowerment,
        20–23
    global acceptance of, 8–9

"good business" of,
    12–18
impact of, 12
marketing, 16–17
positive image, 18–20
qualifiers for, 58–60
universality of, 11
ISO 14001, *see specific*
    standards of ISO 14001
benefits of, 222–223
historical perspective,
    45–46
implementation, 115–116,
    118, 120, 124, 127,
    129
procedure requirements,
    139, 147–148
registration process,
    189–192
scope of, 57–60
Section 4, *see* Section 4
    (ISO 14001)
system changes and,
    159–160
ISO 14004, 142
ISO 14020 Environmental
    Labeling standards,
    214–216

J

Japanese Accreditation Board
    (JAB), 8

Jerai International Park (JIP), 12–13
Job instructions, 53
Job titles, 91–92, 95–96

K

King, Rod, 194
Kopp, Steve, 23
Koretsky, Joseph, 165–168

L

Labeling standards, 210
Labels, environmental, 114, 214–216
Labor unions, 19
Land, environmental concerns, 179–180
Lang, Branda, 22
Language:
  definitions, overview, 60–73
  in environmental manual, 127
  legal requirements and, 89–90
  standard, 48–49
Leadership, commitment and, 25, 115–117
Legal requirements, 89–90

Legislation, *see* Government regulation
Levi Strauss, 16, 212
Licenses, 197
Life-cycle assessment, 91–92, 113, 123–124, 130
Lloyd's of London, 15
Love Canal, 4
Lunch, Rick, 15

M

McDonald's, 213
Macleish, Archibald, 31
Makower, Joel, 24, 31
Management representative, role of, 116, 121
Management review, 107–108
Management review meetings, 203
Manual, environmental:
  contents of, 52, 124–127
  documentation, 114–115
  establishment, 120
Market-driven approach, 30
Marketing:
  credibility in, 214–215
  image development, 16–17, 210, 216–217
  impact of, 212–214
  reputation and, 211–213

Medical equipment
    manufacturers, 118
Mercosur, 36
Mission statement, 118
Monsanto, 212
Munich Re, 15
Mutual fund companies, 16

N

Netherlands, 8, 10
Nippon Petroleum, 19
Nonconformance, 103–104,
    184, 204
Nonconformance Reports
    (NCRs), 204
Normative references, 60
North American Free Trade
    Agreement, 36
North Korea, 35
Norway, 8

O

Objectives, environmental:
  defined, 67, 119–120
  environmental
      performance indicators,
      146–147
  four-stage plan for setting,
      142–143

guidelines for, 140–141
  ranking environmental
      activities, 143–146
  Section 4 requirements
      (ISO 14001), 84–85,
      90–91, 102–103
Odom, William, 210
Opening meeting, 200
Operating procedures,
    121–122
Operational control, 100–101
Organization, defined, 71
Organizational charts, 92

P

Pacific Rim, 36, 225
People's Republic of China,
    19
Performance, environmental,
    67–68
Performance evaluation,
    environmental, 113
Perrier, 4
Perry Johnson, Inc., 177, 192,
    194
Pesticides, 72
Philippines, 8
Pitfalls, avoidance strategies,
    159–168
Planning, questions for,
    160–162

Polaroid, 16
Policy, environmental:
  communication of,
    201–202
  defined, 68
  documentation of, 114–115
  establishment of, 119,
    122–123
  life-cycle thinking,
    123–124
  Section 4 requirements
    (ISO 14001), 79–86
Pollution prevention, 71–73,
  83–84
Population growth, impact of,
  223–224
Preregistration audit,
  196–199
Preventive actions, 103–104,
  154, 203
Prioritizing, objectives and
  targets, 143–145
Probable Risk Assessment
  Model (PRAM), 144
Procedural tests, 102
Procedures:
  defined, 135–136
  environmental
    management
    programs, 147–153
  objectives and targets,
    140–147
  system changes, 154–156
  types of, 136–139

  written, *see* Written
    procedures
Process improvement teams,
  151
Product standards,
  environment aspects,
  114
Public relations, 214

Q

Quality assurance, 162
Quality management system
  (QMS), 86
QS9000, 11

R

Real Goods, 212
Records:
  Section 4 requirements
    (ISO 14001), 104–105
  supporting, 114–115
  types of, 53
Reebok, 16
Registrar:
  function of, 48, 59
  preregistration audit,
    197–198
  selection of, 193–194
Registrar Accreditation Board
  (RAB), 193, 195

Registration audit, internal
    audit compared with, 181
Registration process, ISO
    14001:
    formal steps of, 196–204
    implementation cycle,
       194–196
    overview, 193
    registrar, selection of,
       193–194
Reich, Chuck, 8
Right-to-Know Act, 17
Rockwell International, 8
Russia, 36

S

Safety responsibilities, 93–94
SAGE (Strategic Advisory
    Group on the
    Environment), 39–40
Sato, Yasufumi, 9
Section 4 (ISO 14001):
    checking and corrective
       action, 102–107
    environmental policy,
       79–80
    general requirements, 79
    implementation and
       operation, 92–102
    management review,
       107–108
    planning, 87–92

Seif, James M., 29–30
Seipke, Denise, 176
Self-assurance, 58
Self-declaration, 58–59
Self-determination, 58–59
Senior management, *see* Top
    management
SGS Thomson, 8
"Shall" statements, 47–48,
    87, 119, 125, 137
Sharp Microelectronics
    Technology (SMT), 167
Shroyer, Jon, 167–168
Silent Spring (Carson), 30
Smith, Jack, 20
Smith, Roger, 33
Socially Responsible Investing
    (SRI), 15
Social responsibility, 25
Sony, 8, 19
South Korea, 35
Soviet Union, environment
    degradation in, 35
Spaceship earth, 31
Standard operating
    procedures (SOPs), 52,
    91–92
Starkist, 24
Stewardship, environmental,
    16, 18, 22, 25, 35
Superfund Amendments and
    Reauthorization Act,
    17
Supervision, 165–168

Suppliers, 88, 130
Supporting records, 114–115

T

Target, environmental, *see*
    Objectives,
    environmental
    defined, 68–69
    implementation of,
        119–120
    procedures and, 145–146
    Section 4 requirements
        (ISO 14001), 84–85,
        90–91, 102–103
Target Stores, 16, 212
Technical Advisory Groups
    (TAGs), 41, 80
Technical Committee 207,
    41
Technological advances,
    impact of, 225–228
Texas Instruments, 16
Third World, 42, 224–225
Third-party audit team,
    181–182, 185
Thomson, William, 67
3M Corporation, 10, 13,
    211–213
Three Mile Island, 4
Time lines, 144–145
Time Warner, 16

Top management:
    commitment, 164, 166
    documentation and, 85
    environmental policy and,
        82
    function of, generally, 93,
        107–108, 112, 116,
        122–123, 131, 150
Toshiba Corporation, 8
Total quality management
    (TQM), 6, 222
Toyota, 19
Trading blocks, 36–37
Training:
    for auditors, 173, 176–182
    for employees, 49, 121
    methods of, 153
    needs analysis, in
        registration process,
        201
    registration requirements,
        195
    Section 4 requirements
        (ISO 14001), 94–96
Train-track syndrome,
    175

U

Ukraine, 36
Umbrella procedures,
    136–138

United Kingdom
    Accreditation Service
    (UKAS), 191
United Nations:
  Agenda 21, 19, 40
  Environmental Program,
    37
U.S. Technical Advisory
    Group (TAG), 41
Updating standards, 89, 154

V

Vendors, 71, 130
Viacom, 16, 212
Vision, 118, 131, 209
Volvo, 8

W

Water, environmental
    concerns, 178–179

"We do" statements, 125
West Germany, 35
"What if" attitude, 89
Working Assets Long
    Distance, 213
Work instructions, 114–115,
    136, 138–139, 202
Work records, 53
World Bank, 14–15, 224
World Business Council for
    Sustainable
    Development, 13
World Commission on
    Environment and
    Development, 37–38
Written procedures:
  documentation, 114–115
  establishment of, 118–120
  guidelines for, 137–138

X

Xerox, 13, 16